THE LAST

Ten Signs of the End of the Age

GENERATION

D0681183

by
Jack Kinsella

True Potential Publishing, Inc.
Travelers Rest, SC

True Potential Publishing, Inc.
P.O. Box 904
Travelers Rest, SC 29690
Visit our website at www.tppress.com

Scripture quotations in this volume are from the King James Version of the Bible unless specifically credited to another source.

ISBN 978-0-9767811-8-9

Library of Congress Control Number: 2007927927

1. Bible-Prophecies-Messianic. 2. Bible-Prophesies-End of the world. 3. Eschatology. 4. Eschatology-Israel. I Title.

Printed in the United States of America

To my beloved wife and partner in all things, Gayle, without whom I would be but an empty shell of a man. And of course, to my Lord and Savior, Jesus Christ of Nazareth.

ACKNOWLEDGMENTS:

It is difficult to acknowledge all the people who help make this book possible, but even a partial and incomplete list must include my mentor, best friend and spiritual father, Hal Lindsey; my publisher, editor and advisor, Steve Spillman; my webmaster and son-in-law Mike Velemirovich; the many members of my Omega Letter internet "family" -- and Rick White, Captain John Kurek and Becky Hobgood, and the rest of "locals" of Atlantic Beach, NC, who sheltered and nurtured me throughout the process.

CONTENTS

Words as Weapons
Dinner for One
He Who Owns the News, Makes the News
"It's Ok. Soothe Me…"

"Armageddon" for the Dark Continent?
The Rise of the Superbugs
Red Flags Everywhere
Rocking the House
"And All the Fishes in the Sea"
"Behold, A Black Horse"
Guardian Polar Bears and Fat Mice

Space Rocks, Air Bags and Armageddon
2050 Party Over - Out of Time
Scared Yet?
New Age Masquerading as News
"Distress of Nations"
UN Report: The Beginning of Sorrows
The Earth is Bi-Polar!
Will the Toilets Flush Backwards?
Spots Before Our Eyes
"The Sky is Falling"
Earthquakes Famines and Wars

The King's Dream
Future History from the Distant Past
The Beast that Was, is Not and Yet is
Mystery Babylon
The Political Beast
The Religious "Beast"
The Benelux Treaty
Coincidences Abound
The Big Picture

What Are The Odds?

FOREWORD

Jack Kinsella and I have worked together as friends and colleagues for more than 15 years. We have reported the contemporary news and related it to the prophecies of the Bible that apply to the events that lead to the imminent return of Jesus Christ to Planet Earth.

I have witnessed first hand the great spiritual gifts with which God has endowed Kinsella. He has a comprehensive knowledge of Bible prophecy. He also has a keen grasp of history. Wedded to this is an ability to write in an investigative reporter style that makes him both interesting and easy to understand.

I just finished reading his book, *The Last Generation*. I believe it is a milestone in the field of Bible prophecy. It is a terrific, exciting account of how today's news is fitting precisely into the scenario of predicted events that immediately precede the Return of Jesus Christ. He gives many convincing evidences that Bible prophecies made thousands of years ago are indeed being fulfilled before our eyes.

It is a must read. Whether you are religious or non-religious – believer or skeptic – I believe you will find Kinsella's book fascinating. For many, it will be life changing.

Dr. Hal Lindsey

INTRODUCTION

> And as He sat upon the mount of Olives, the disciples
> came unto Him privately, saying, Tell us, when shall
> these things be? and what shall be the sign of Thy
> coming, and of the end of the world?
>
> (Matthew 24:3)

For two thousand years, scholars, theologians, skeptics and
critics have dissected both that question and its answer. To
the faithful, it is Divine prophecy intended to offer comfort
and wisdom to the generation that would see its fulfillment.

To the critics and skeptics, it is offered as evidence that the
Bible is a book of myths. They argue that every generation
thought they were the ones that would see the "end of the
world" (the return of Christ) but, look! We're still here!
Hardly an original argument, but one that has endured
through the ages.

> Knowing this first, that there shall come in the last
> days scoffers, walking after their own lusts, And
> saying, Where is the promise of His coming? for since
> the fathers fell asleep, all things continue as they were
> from the beginning of the creation.
>
> (II Peter 3:3,4)

The Apostle Peter reminds his readers that they laughed
when Noah built his ark ... until it started to rain. Peter
defines the logic of accepting the absence of evidence as
itself being evidence as "willing ignorance" (II Peter 3:5).

From that perspective, it is not coincidental that the first warning Jesus gave His disciples in answer to their question was, "Take heed that no man deceive you" (Matthew 24:4).

Evidence of a Plan

Jesus next warned His disciples, "...ye shall hear of wars and rumours of wars," adding, "...see that ye be not troubled: for all these things must come to pass, but the end is not yet" (Matthew 24:6).

The twentieth century is divided by its wars; pre-World War I, post-World War I, pre-World War II, post World War II, the Cold War, and the post Cold-War. The First World War was so ferocious and bloody that it earned the appellation, "The War to End All Wars." The carnage claimed the lives of more than thirty-eight million people worldwide. Entire nations were reduced to rubble. The cream of a generation perished on the battlefields of Europe. "Never again!" shouted the survivors.

Despite the best efforts of the *League of Nations* created to fulfill that promise, the madness once again overspread the globe less than a generation later. This time, the carnage claimed almost twice as many lives worldwide as the last one had. It concluded with the introduction of the world's first use of nuclear weapons, and established America as the greatest military power the world had ever known.

In 1948, as the surviving Jews of Hitler's madness declared the existence of the State of Israel, Russia declared a blockade of West Berlin, which was at the time under control of the post-war Victorious Powers. The United States launched a massive airlift of supplies into Berlin, eventually breaking the blockade and officially kicking off the ultimate "rumor of war," the Cold War.

Jesus intimated that the wars and rumors of wars were a

necessary part of an unfolding plan; hence His admonition, "see that yet not be troubled." He explained, "...for all these things must come to pass, but the end is not yet." Jesus was asked of the signs of the end. In His response, He said these were signs, but the end is not yet. Is there a relevant cause and effect at work here?

It is logical to infer that these wars were both necessary to a plan, and that they signaled, not the end, but the beginning of the end. Among the consequences of the *War to End All Wars* were the collapse of the Ottoman Empire and the occupation of the Holy Land by the British. In 1917, the British Parliament adopted the Balfour Declaration that declared the newly acquired territory of Palestine as the "homeland of the Jews."

The carnage of the Holocaust turned the surviving Jews of Europe into refugees; their property confiscated, the wealth plundered. They had nowhere to go but Palestine. The hardships they endured under their Nazi tormentors steeled them for the hardships ahead.

The generation of Jews that settled Israel withstood five separate efforts by the combined Arab world to annihilate them, each time, emerging from battle in possession of a larger piece of the Promised Land. And the ultimate "rumor of war" forced Israel's alliance with the Western world when the Soviets began setting up client states in the Middle East.

The entire focus of Bible prophecy in the last days demands the existence of a Jewish State called "Israel." Israel plays a central role in the unfolding of all Bible prophecy in the last days. The unintended consequences of two wars and what turned out to be a "rumor of war" was the Western acquisition of the Land of Promise, the forced relocation of European Jewry to that land, and Israel's necessary alliance to the United States.

Coincidence? Or cause and effect?

Beginning of Sorrows

> For nation shall rise against nation, and kingdom against kingdom: and there shall be famines, and pestilences, and earthquakes, in divers places. All these are the beginning of sorrows.
>
> (Matthew 24:7-8)

Jesus warned that these signs were the "beginnings of sorrows." *Sorrows* is a reference to birth pangs (Genesis 3:16 "...in sorrow thou shalt bring forth children;"). Jesus used an analogy that would remain constant throughout human history. We still time labor pains. As the time approaches, the labor pains increase in both frequency and intensity.

Wars, famines and "pestilences" (plagues) have always been part of the human condition. Until mankind declared them obsolete in the mid-twentieth century. We declared war on wars, setting up the United Nations as the preferred forum for settling national differences. And for a time, it worked as advertised.

We declared war on poverty and set up programs to bring food to deprived nations and set up international agencies to help develop underprivileged nations. We declared war on disease, and all but eradicated deadly epidemics of bubonic plague, tuberculosis, polio, malaria, leprosy and smallpox. We developed antibiotics to prevent their recurrence.

We made real progress, and it looked for a while as if we might actually stamp out mankind's ancient scourges.

But that was before the appearance of antibiotic resistant "superbugs". And new, unknown diseases like HIV, AIDS and SARS ... and a host of other formerly unheard of epidemics.

Bird flu made its appearance in Asia in the twenty-first century and with it, the specter of a global pandemic that the experts estimate could kill tens (maybe hundreds) of millions of people. Of those infected so far, more than half have died, giving it a mortality rate of almost 60 percent.

Rocking the House

There remains a huge debate raging over global warming. Actually, it isn't even accurate to call it a debate over global warming. Few are arguing that global warming doesn't exist. Some are arguing that it is merely a normal part of global weather pattern cycles, but those arguments are rapidly losing credibility in the face of empirical evidence to the contrary.

What is at the heart of the debate is the cause. Most blame the United States and insist that it accept responsibility for its cleanup, as demanded by the Kyoto Treaty.

An equally strong argument exists for laying the blame at the Soviet Union's doorstep. It used Eastern Europe as a toxic waste dump. It polluted with impunity for sixty years, and then left the mess untouched after its collapse.

China is among the world's worst polluters, along with having one of the world's largest populations to clean up after.

But global warming and pollution don't account for the rest of the planetary upheaval; the earthquakes, solar flares, changes to the earth's magnetic fields, and so on and so forth.

The Last Generation

The earthquake that ushered in 2005 was so powerful that it reshaped the earth's surface, disrupted the space-time continuum; the entire planet was still vibrating like a tuning fork as the ball came down at Times Square.

There were 23,617 earthquakes world-wide in 2005 that claimed more than 83,000 lives. That is up from 16,612 in 1990; part of an upward trend that is still continuing.

Geopolitically, the 21st century so far has been marked by belligerency and war. There is the Iraq War. The Afghanistan War. The war on terror. The culture wars. The Red State/Blue State political war. The Iran nuclear crisis is the new century's offering for the "rumor of war" category.

And where open war hasn't erupted, ethnic unrest threatens to spark it at almost any moment.

Jesus was asked by His disciples what "signs" would be given in advance of His return.

He spoke of wars and rumors of wars, famines, earthquakes, saying, "And great earthquakes shall be in divers places, and famines, and pestilences; and fearful sights and great signs shall there be from heaven" (Luke 21:11).

He warned:

> And there shall be signs in the sun, and in the moon, and in the stars; and upon the earth distress of nations, with perplexity; the sea and the waves roaring; Men's hearts failing them for fear, and for looking after those things which are coming on the earth: for the powers of heaven shall be shaken.
>
> (Luke 21:25-26)

He said to the generation that would witness these signs, "when these things begin to come to pass, then look up, and lift up your heads; for your redemption draweth nigh" (Luke 21:28).

I am struck with renewed awe with how perfectly it all conforms to Jesus' outline for a single generation, somewhere in time. While these events have always been part of the human condition, new records shatter like old glass with each passing year. And, as you will see, this is only the tip of the iceberg.

> So likewise ye, when ye shall see all these things, know that it is near, even at the doors. Verily I say unto you, This generation shall not pass, till all these things be fulfilled.
>
> (Matthew 24:33-34)

CHAPTER ONE

THE RESTORATION OF ISRAEL

The Fig Tree

> Therefore prophesy and say unto them, Thus saith the Lord GOD; Behold, O my people, I will open your graves, and cause you to come up out of your graves, and bring you into the land of Israel.... Say unto them, Thus saith the Lord GOD; Behold, I will take the stick of Joseph, which is in the hand of Ephraim, and the tribes of Israel his fellows, and will put them with him, even with the stick of Judah, and make them one stick, and they shall be one in mine hand.... And I will make them one nation in the land upon the mountains of Israel; and one king shall be king to them all: and they shall be no more two nations, neither shall they be divided into two kingdoms any more at all.
>
> (Ezekiel 37:12, 19-20, 22)

One of the most clear and undeniable signs of the last days is the restoration of Israel. It is an event unique in the annals of human history.

The Jewish culture, unlike other cultures of antiquity, was never absorbed by its many conquerors. Even after being divided, scattered across the centuries and throughout the world, without land or flag, the Jewish nation survived.

Abram the Idol-Maker

Abram was the son of a Chaldean idol maker named Terah who lived in the land of Ur, located about 200 miles south of modern Baghdad. According to Jewish tradition, one day, Abram secretly smashed all his father's idols.

When an enraged Terah asked who had committed this outrage, Abram told his father that one of the idols jumped up, grabbed a stick and went on a rampage.

"That's impossible," exclaimed Terah. "They are but statues made of stone and wood."

"Why, then," Abram asked, "do we worship them?"

Abram was commanded by God to "Get thee out of thy country, and from thy kindred, and from thy father's house, unto a land that I will show thee" (Genesis 12:1).

Abram packed up his family and made the journey to the Land of Canaan on the plain of Moreh.

> And the LORD appeared unto Abram, and said, Unto thy seed will I give this land: and there builded he an altar unto the LORD, who appeared unto him.
>
> (Genesis 12:7)

God later made a covenant with Abram, whose name He changed to Abraham, and promised him that his descendants would inherit the land of Canaan forever. But Abraham's descendants broke that covenant, and as a consequence, endured centuries of warfare, disaster, conquest and catastrophe.

Ultimately, they were ordered into exile by the Romans in A.D. 70, after which they wandered the earth, living as guests in whatever country would host them.

But God had promised the Jews that, despite the odds, He would re-gather them into the Land of Promise in the last days.

Without nation, land or flag, persecuted on all sides, strangers even after generations in their host nations, the Jews waited for the fulfillment of the Promise; each Passover praying, "Next year, in Jerusalem."

May 14, 1948, almost two thousand years after they were dispossessed from their ancestral homeland, David Ben-Gurion, as its first prime minister, announced the re-establishment of a Jewish state called "Israel".

Think this through for a moment. Broken into small groups, many unaware of the existence of others like them, the Jews survived. Across the span of centuries, scattered throughout hundreds of countries; their culture, religion, unique dietary laws, customs and traditions remained intact.

Despite the best efforts of the rest of the world to bring about their destruction through periodic massacres, forced conversions and pogrom after pogrom, the Jews survived.

Today, the state of Israel is home to Jews from every country, speaking 86 languages.

In each adopted language, they heard the story of the Exodus. In each host country, sometimes at risk of death, they kept the Passover. When they came home to the Promised Land, they found other Jews, telling the story of the Exodus, each in their own language.

And it was the same story - because they were the same people.

From the Ends of the Earth

> But now thus saith the LORD that created thee, O Jacob, and He that formed thee, O Israel, Fear not: for I have redeemed thee, I have called thee by thy name; thou art Mine.
>
> (Isaiah 43:1)

King Nebuchadnezzar of Babylon laid siege to the Kingdom of Judah for almost twenty years before capturing the city of Jerusalem and the Temple treasures in 586 B.C., taking the cream of Israeli society captive and leaving what remained in ruins.

Babylon and its conquered territories later fell to the Medo-Persian Empire. Cyrus, king of Persia, eventually released the Hebrew captives and authorized the rebuilding of Jerusalem and the Temple.

Most scholars place Isaiah Chapters 40-55 during the time the Babylonian captivity. The Book of Isaiah is one of the richest sources of what is known as *dual fulfillment* prophecy in Scripture.

Dual-fulfillment refers to prophecies that were fulfilled in part during the period of history in which they were written, with the remainder to be fulfilled on a grander scale at some later point in history.

Isaiah 43 is an excellent example of *dual fulfillment* prophecy. Verses one through seven address the ingathering of the exiles, which took place in part, following Persian King Ahasuerus Longimanus' decree to rebuild the city and sanctuary.

But these verses also prefigure a complete ingathering of exiles from the "from the ends the earth" in the last days.

Isaiah 43:8-9 is another example of *dual-fulfillment* prophecy:

> Bring forth the blind people that have eyes, and the deaf that have ears. Ye are My witnesses, saith the LORD, and My Servant whom I have chosen: that ye may know and believe Me, and understand that I am He: before Me there was no God formed, neither shall there be after Me.

While God is addressing the Jews in Babylonian captivity, He also includes the promise of a Redeemer; One Who gives sight to the blind and hearing to the deaf. He includes in this scripture, a challenge to all those who would claim another god.

> Ye are My witnesses, saith the LORD, and My servant whom I have chosen: that ye may know and believe Me, and understand that I am He: before Me there was no God formed, neither shall there be after Me. I, even I, am the LORD; and beside Me there is no Saviour.

> (Isaiah 43:10-11)

This is a clear reference to the coming Messiah, Whom John 1:1-3 would reveal as the Creator of the Universe:

> In the beginning was the Word, and the Word was with God, and the Word was God. The same was in the beginning with God. All things were made by Him; and without Him was not any thing made that was made.

The "Word" (Jesus) was God, and as such, was with God in the beginning, and it was He, Jesus, Who was the Creator of the physical universe.

In this passage of Isaiah, we find history, (Creation) and three separate prophecies; the promise of Judah's return from captivity in Babylon (fulfilled in 445 B.C.), the coming of the Messiah (fulfilled some 500 years later), and the ultimate re-gathering of Israel into their own land in the last days (in the process of being fulfilled today).

The re-gathering in Isaiah's day was only a partial fulfillment, since only the Jews of Judah were restored by Ahasuerus. The ten northern tribes of the Kingdom of Israel were taken into exile by Sargon the Assyrian in 702 B.C., after which they disappeared from history.

After the Israelites were conquered and scattered, only the Jews of Judah remained. Judah was then taken into exile by the Babylonians and later restored to the Promised Land by the Persians.

Isaiah's ultimate prophetic re-gathering is not the re-gathering of the Jews of Judah, but of the whole nation of Israel.

"For I am the LORD thy God, the Holy One of *Israel*, thy Saviour: I gave Egypt for thy ransom, Ethiopia and Seba for thee" (Isaiah 43:3).

Operation Solomon

Israel launched "Operation Solomon" in 1991. It was a massive, one-day airlift of 14,000 Ethiopian Jews to Israel in the midst of the Ethiopian Civil War.

> From beyond the rivers of Ethiopia my suppliants, even the daughter of my dispersed, shall bring mine offering. In that day shalt thou not be ashamed for all thy doings, wherein thou hast transgressed against me: for then I will take away out of the midst of thee them that rejoice in thy pride, and thou shalt no more be haughty because of my holy mountain.
>
> (Zephaniah 3:10-11)

One can search the annals of history in vain for another people like the Jews. No other people of antiquity have survived into modern times under such circumstances.

There are no Amalekites, Jebusites or Canaanites. These ancient tribes may have descendants, but they are not a *people*. By contrast, many Jews can trace their ancestry back to the time of Herod's Temple.

Much of the history of the Jews was written in advance, including their return to the land of Promise in the last generation.

> And the LORD shall scatter you among the nations, and ye shall be left few in number among the heathen, whither the LORD shall lead you. And there ye shall serve gods, the work of men's hands, wood and stone, which neither see, nor hear, nor eat, nor smell. When thou art in tribulation, and all these things are come upon thee, [even] in the latter days, if thou turn to the LORD thy God, and shalt be obedient unto his voice; (For the LORD thy God [is] a merciful God;) he will not forsake thee, neither destroy thee, nor forget the covenant of thy fathers which he sware unto them.
>
> (Deuteronomy 4:27-28, 30-31)

As Moses predicted, the Jews were scattered and persecuted, but, in the "latter days" have been restored for the express purpose of accomplishing their national redemption. Isaiah predicted:

> And it shall come to pass in that day, that the Lord shall set his hand again the second time to recover the remnant of his people, which shall be left, from Assyria, and from Egypt, and from Pathros, and from Cush, and from Elam, and from Shinar, and from Hamath, and from the islands of the sea.
>
> (Isaiah 11:11)

> For, lo, the days come, saith the LORD, that I will bring again the captivity of my people Israel and Judah, saith the LORD: and I will cause them to return to the land that I gave to their fathers, and they shall possess it.
>
> Jeremiah 30:3

> For, behold, in those days, and in that time, when I shall bring again the captivity of Judah and Jerusalem, I will also gather all nations, and will bring them down into the valley of Jehoshaphat, and will plead with them there for my people and [for] my heritage Israel, whom they have scattered among the nations, and parted my land.
>
> Joel 3:1-2

> In that day will I raise up the tabernacle of David that is fallen, and close up the breaches thereof; and I will raise up his ruins, and I will build it as in the days of old:
>
> Amos 9:11

The Bnei Menashi

Israel's chief counsel of rabbis certified a group of some seven thousand inhabitants of the remote northeastern Indian states of Mizoram and Minapur as members of the Bnei Menashe; one of the ten tribes of Israel that were lost to history after being sent into exile by the Assyrians in 702B.C..

The first of those newly-certified Jewish exiles began returning to Israel in late 2006 in what the Jewish rabbis called "a fulfillment of Bible prophecy."

Michael Jankelowitz, spokesman for the Jerusalem-based *Jewish Agency*, which coordinated the Indians' arrival, said, "they have lived a Jewish way of life for decades";

including keeping Saturday as the Sabbath and observing Jewish dietary laws.

The tale of how the community's ancestors came to India's northeast, sandwiched between Bangladesh and Myanmar, is fascinating. Exiled by the Assyrians, the tribe was apparently forced east through Afghanistan and China before settling in what is now India's north-east.

Rabbi Avihayil, who discovered the Menashe, says he learned of them back in 1979; after two years of studying their history and traditions, he identified them as members of the lost tribe. Among the telltale signs, he said, were traditions resembling those of the ancient Israelites; including establishing places of refuge for those who had killed another by mistake.

Rabbi Avihayil said his research revealed that the descendants of Menasseh also practiced circumcision, albeit with sharpened flint rather than a knife. In 1982, Rabbi Avihayil traveled to India, where he met the Bnei Menashi. In 1989 he sent a religious official to convert 24 people to Judaism.

The ingathering of Jews from exile is a central theme of the last days:

> ...I will bring thy seed from the east, and gather thee from the west; I will say to the north, Give up; and to the south, Keep not back: bring My sons from far, and My daughters from the ends of the earth.

> (Isaiah 43:5-6)

By Rabbi Avihayil's estimate, there are tens of millions of descendants of the lost tribes of Israel living in Japan, Afghanistan, Pakistan, China, Thailand and Burma.[1]

The Last Generation

"It is not our task to bring all of the ten tribes back, that is the task of the Messiah," he said. "But it is our task, before the Messiah comes, to create an opening in this matter."

The ingathering is in process. The ten lost tribes of Israel are rediscovering their Jewish history in places throughout the world, from east to west, north to south, exactly as prophesied, and are being "lifted up" and put back down again in their own land.

Just in time for the expected Messiah of the re-gathered Israel.

Evidence of Perfect Planning

It seems pretty clear that Israel's history was carefully planned according to a particular purpose. Take a second to think it through.

Foretelling the future of an entire nation is more than a good guess. Every person in every generation must cooperate exactly; from Abraham forward.

If Moses' mother hadn't put him in a basket, there'd be no Exodus. Moses' great-grandparents could have only married each other, or there'd been no Moses.

And what if Habakkuk's great-great-great-grandfather decided to be a bachelor? Every single individual choice throughout history - ancient and modern - had to be exactly the right choice for the future to work out according to prophecy.

What if David Ben-Gurion had been killed during WWII or if Israeli Founding Father Abba Eban had decided to remain in the British Army, or if Golda Meir had stayed in Chicago? Modern Israel might not exist.

Meticulous details, maybe - but God said that modern Israel *would* exist in the last days.

Personal Witness

> In accordance with our plan a letter from Weitzman to Truman had been sent on May 13 asking him to recognize the new state. The expected infant was still nameless, since the Zionist leaders were still, characteristically, arguing over the name (should it be "Judea," "Zion," what about "Israel"?). Weitzman, for the first time in history, was asking for a nameless state to be recognized. [2]

> And say unto them, Thus saith the Lord GOD; Behold, I will take the children of Israel from among the heathen, whither they be gone, and will gather them on every side, and bring them into their own land: And I will make them one nation in the land upon the mountains of Israel; and one king shall be king to them all: and they shall be no more two nations, neither shall they be divided into two kingdoms any more at all.

> (Ezekiel 37:21-22)

Abba Eban was Israel's first representative to the United Nations, even before there was a state of Israel. Prior to declaring statehood, Eban was the Jewish Relief Agency's official representative to the UN.

Eban served in the twin capacity of Israeli Ambassador to the UN and Israeli Ambassador to the US, before becoming Israel's foreign minister.

Abba Eban was present for every major event in the life of the modern Jewish State from its inception until he left the Knesset in 1988.

Eban was known for his blunt honesty and no-nonsense attitude, having once told the UN General Assembly:

> If Algeria introduced a resolution declaring that the earth was flat and that Israel had flattened it, it would pass by a vote of 164 to 13 with 26 abstentions.

He had a way of putting things into perspective unmatched by his contemporaries. Speaking of the 1967 Six-Day War, Eban quipped; "I think that this is the first war in history that on the morrow the victors sued for peace and the vanquished called for unconditional surrender."

Eban recounts that the Soviet Union, initially, enthusiastically supported the establishment of a Jewish State, while the United States very nearly withheld recognition, which would have doomed Israel to stillbirth.

"I Won't Vote For You"

President Truman, a crusty mid-Westerner with no particular love for the Jews, fought a pitched battle with Secretary of State George C Marshall, who told Truman in blunt terms; "They don't deserve a state, they have stolen that country. If you give this recognition, Mr. President, I may not vote for you in the next election."

In the end, Truman decided against the expressed and united opinion of his cabinet. He sent a cable to Tel Aviv, assuring David Ben-Gurion of the US intention to recognize the new Jewish state. On May 14, Joseph Cohn, Chaim Weitzman's personal secretary, was dispatched to Washington to inform Truman that the name of the state he was about to recognize would be "Israel."

As it grew apparent that the new Jewish state was looking westward to America, instead of east toward Moscow for its principle political alliances, the Soviets soured on the new state and turned instead to support Israel's Arab enemies.

Among the punitive policies adopted by the Kremlin was a complete ban on emigration by Soviet-bloc Jews to the Jewish state.

Israel's existence is a miracle accomplished by God, specifically as He said it would be accomplished. Specifically when He intended - in the last days. When the time came, the world convulsed into World War II, and regurgitated the nation it had been holding captive until the appointed time.

Three years after the Holocaust, on May 14, 1948, Israel raised her flag. For the first time since 702 B.C., there was a place in the world called Israel and a home for the Jews.

> And they shall dwell in the land that I have given unto Jacob my servant, wherein your fathers have dwelt; and they shall dwell therein, even they, and their children, and their children's children for ever: and my servant David shall be their prince for ever. My tabernacle also shall be with them: yea, I will be their God, and they shall be my people. And the heathen shall know that I the LORD do sanctify Israel, when my sanctuary shall be in the midst of them for evermore.
>
> (Ezekiel 37:25, 27-28)

There is no story like Israel's. There is no nation like Israel. God said, "I found Israel like grapes in the wilderness; I saw your fathers as the firstripe in the fig tree at her first time…" (Hosea 9:10).

The Chosen People

> And in that day will I make Jerusalem a burdensome stone for all people: all that burden themselves with it shall be cut in pieces, though all the people of the earth be gathered together against it.

> Zechariah 12:3

For most of Israel's existence, it seemed unlikely that "all the people of the earth" would gather against it over the issue of Jerusalem. It is clear enough that anti-Semitism is alive and well on Planet Earth and that a universal constant in human history seems to be hatred of the Jews, for no other offense than *being* Jews.

The reason why is clear. God said that is how it would be; as part of His overall plan for Israel's national redemption on the last day.

> ...Jerusalem, and the cities of Judah, and the kings thereof, and the princes thereof, to make them a desolation, an astonishment, an hissing, and a curse; as it is this day;

> (Jeremiah 25:18)

Israel's history, from the time of Christ until the final generation, was predicted in a single sentence by the prophet Jeremiah.

> I will persecute them with the sword, with the famine, and with the pestilence, and will deliver them to be removed to all the kingdoms of the earth, to be a curse, and an astonishment, and an hissing, and a reproach, among all the nations whither I have driven them:

> (29:18)

But Isaiah prophesied that, in the last days:

> I will bring thy seed from the east, and gather thee
> from the west; I will say to the north, Give up; and to
> the south, Keep not back: bring My sons from far, and
> My daughters from the ends of the earth; Even every
> one that is called by My Name: for I have created him
> for My glory, I have formed him; yea, I have made
> him.

(Isaiah 43:5-7)

Jews have been born, lived and died in every country on earth, but their birth nation was never more than a temporary "host" country.

In any country where Jews lived, they were merely "German Jews" or "Iraqi Jews" or "British Jews," subject to periodic pogroms, deportations or forced conversions. The first country on earth to extend full citizenship rights to Jews was the United States of America.

Israel is universally hated, not for anything the Jews have actually done to anybody, but for whom they claim to be; "God's Chosen People."

Even those who don't believe in God hate the Jews for their claimed "special relationship" but no group in history has demonstrated their hate for the Jews more than those who claim to the title of "Christian".

It is no wonder that Jews fear and distrust Christians. For two thousand years, they were persecuted and executed under the shadow of the Cross. Throughout the Middle Ages, they were persecuted as "Christ-killers." The Nazis claimed the Holocaust as a holy Christian mission to rid the world of Jews.

But those who revile the Jews for claiming the title of "God's Chosen People" don't understand for what *purpose* God chose the Jews.

> For I would not, brethren, that ye should be ignorant of this mystery, lest ye should be wise in your own conceits; that blindness in part is happened to Israel, until the fulness of the Gentiles be come in.

(Romans 11:25)

The Apostle Paul makes it clear that God chose to impose spiritual blindness on Israel for the sake of the Gentiles. Consider this. Had the Jews accepted Christ at His first advent, the Church would never have existed.

As we've seen, people who deny Christ will justify their anti-Semitism using the same libel.

The Libelous "Christ-Killer" Label

Why do I say it is a "libel" - a historical slander? After all, when Pilate washed his hands of responsibility for the execution of Jesus, saying, "I am innocent of the blood of this just Person: see ye to it," the Jewish mob chanted in reply, "His blood be on us, and on our children" (Mathew 27:24-25).

Jesus was tried and convicted by the Jewish Supreme Court, the Sanhedrin, in an illegal trial in which no fewer than thirteen Jewish laws were broken. Since the Jews, being an occupied province of Rome, were not sovereign, their courts could not order an execution. This is why they took the case to Pilate in the first place.

So, if the Jews themselves, following an illegal trial, had Jesus murdered at the hands of an unwilling occupation authority that would have preferred to have released Him, why is it a *libel* to call Jews "Christ-killers"?

Jesus told His disciples:

> Therefore doth My Father love Me, because I lay down My life, that I might take it again. No man taketh it from Me, but I lay it down of Myself. I have power to lay it down, and I have power to take it again.

(John 10:17-18)

No man *could* have taken Jesus' life. Not Pilate, not the Jews, not Satan or his legions.

When Satan appeared in the wilderness to tempt Jesus, he quoted Psalms 91:11-12:

> For He shall give His angels charge over Thee, to keep Thee in all thy ways. They shall bear Thee up in their hands, lest thou dash Thy foot against a stone.

If Jesus alone had the power lay down His life, and that no man could *take* it, then the crime cannot be laid to any human being's charge. Indeed, at the cross Jesus cried, "Father, forgive them; for they know not what they do" (Luke 23:34).

If Jesus pronounced their forgiveness at the cross for participating in a pre-ordained and necessary sacrifice in which Jesus *voluntarily* laid down His life as a propitiation for all sin, how then, can the modern Jews be responsible for the sins of their fathers?

Especially when the One against Whom they sinned had already forgiven them at the cross for their participation?

Doing God "Service"

Jesus tells His disciples (all Jews of Israel);

> These things have I spoken unto you, that ye should not be offended. They shall put you out of the synagogues: yea, the time cometh, that whosoever killeth you will think that he doeth God service.
>
> (John 16:1-2)

What an incredible prophecy! Not only were the Jews put out of the synagogues at some point in history in virtually every country they had adopted, the persecution of the Jews was always for the specific crime of being the "killers of Christ."

History is filled with stories of pogroms, confiscations, expulsions, attempted genocide and persecutions against Jews; all in the name of Christ. In every case, it was presented as "doing God a service" by avenging Christ's murder.

To the nations of the world, the existence of Israel is a thorn in their collective side - because Israel is a thorn in the side of the *god* of this world. Satan has thrown everything he could at the Jews for two thousand years, trying to wipe them from the face of the earth and break God's prophetic promise of Israel's national redemption in the last days.

The survival of the Jew and the restoration of Israel to the Promised Land is proof positive that God remains on the Throne and that these are the last days. His Word will *not* return to Him void. All the chaos and terror of the world notwithstanding, history continues to go according to His plan.

"But these things have I told you, that *when the time shall come*, ye may remember that I told you of them."[3] (John 16:4).

Are Israelis *Really* Biblical Jews?

Many times have I heard people say something like: *The Jews today don't have a drop of Abrahamic blood.* Or that, *the Jews have no racial or historical connection to the Bible and Palestine.*

Some Christians explain the Jews' identity by saying:

> The Jews (Israel) are people who missed (rejected) the coming of the Messiah and thus were cast aside by God, and so now God deals with the Gentiles.

Arab historian Jarid al-Kidwa told an Arab TV audience:

> ...all the events surrounding Kings Saul, David and Rehoboam occurred in Yemen, and no Hebrew remnants were found in Israel, for a very simple reason - because they were never here.[4]

Al-Kidwa continued:

> Most of the Khazars (a Turkish tribe that converted to Judaism in medieval times) are the Ashkenazic Jews who arrived in Palestine. As Allah is my witness, in my blood flows more of the Children of Israel and the ancient Hebrews than in the blood of Ariel Sharon and Benjamin Netanyahu.

According to the Israeli newspaper Ha'aretz, al-Kidwa also said:

> The stories of the Torah and the Bible did not take place in the Land of Israel - they occurred in the Arabian Peninsula, primarily in Yemen. The identity of our father Ibrahim (Abraham) who is mentioned in

the Koran is clear. From the Koran's description of him it arises that he lived in the southern Hejaz (Saudi Arabia), near Mecca.[5]

Most of those who oppose Israel, and especially those Christians who think spiritual Israel is really the Church, include these and similar arguments to support their view. If true, it would bolster the Arab claim to all of Israel and renew global opposition to a "Jewish" state under the old "Zionism is racism" argument.

If today's Jews aren't descended from Abraham, but are instead a mixed race of people whose only common connection is religion, then they are not a "nation" in any identifiable sense. They are instead religious zealots who usurped a Biblical promise in order to steal land from the Arabs based on a fraudulent claim.

The Bible promised the land to the *seed of Abraham* - his physical descendants through his son Isaac to whom the land was promised.

If modern-day Jews are not Abraham's literal seed, but merely the descendants of Jewish converts and followers of Judaic tradition, then the Israeli claim to the land of Israel is false.

Abraham's blessing passed from Isaac to Jacob:

> And give thee the blessing of Abraham, to thee, and to thy seed with thee; that thou mayest inherit the land wherein thou art a stranger, which God gave unto Abraham.

> (Genesis 28:4)

Clearly, if modern Israel isn't the physical and literal seed of Abraham, then Israel's claim to the Land of Promise is a fraud. And our support of Israel on the grounds they are God's Chosen is built on a lie.

Israel's Genetic Priests

The Bible says that in the last days, the seed of Abraham, Isaac and Jacob would return to the "mountains of Israel, which have always been waste" and the nation of Israel would be reborn, "in a day" (Isaiah 66:8).

According to Bible prophecy, during the reign of the antichrist, the Temple will be rebuilt and full temple worship restored. But, in order for temple worship to resume, Jewish religious law requires that the Temple first be ritually cleansed.

According to Levitical law, the only way the Temple area can be ritually restored is by the application of the ashes of a red heifer by an undefiled Cohanim priest. A Cohanim must meet strict bloodline requirements, including direct descendancy from Aaron, the brother of Moses.

So we have several problems here that must be solved before the Tribulation Period begins.

1. Only ethnic Jews, not merely religious Jews, qualify to inherit the Land of Promise. For this to be the last generation, the Jews of Israel *must* be the physical descendants of Abraham, Isaac, Jacob and Moses.
2. To ritually cleanse the Temple, only an ethnic descendant of Aaron, brother of Moses, is qualified to perform the ceremony.
3. This descendant must not be ritually defiled himself.

The Bible says that the Jewish priesthood, the Cohanim, began 3000 years ago when God anointed Aaron, brother of Moses, to be Israel's High Priest.

> And they shall be upon Aaron, and upon his sons, when they come in unto the tabernacle of the congregation, or when they come near unto the altar to minister in the holy place; that they bear not iniquity, and die: it shall be a statute for ever unto him and his seed after him. ...And thou shalt anoint Aaron and his sons, and consecrate them, that they may minister unto me in the priest's office.

> (Exodus 28:43, 30:30)

The title of Cohen is paternally inherited. Most Jewish men surnamed Cohen are also Cohanim, but so are many men with other surnames.

Recently, a genetic study of modern-day Cohanim has provided the first scientific evidence supporting the oral tradition of an ancient priestly lineage.

Karl Skorecki, a physician who studies the genetics of kidney disease at the Technion in Haifa, Israel, as well as colleagues in London and the United States realized that they could study the lineage of priests by looking at the Y chromosome, which only men carry.

Unlike all other chromosomes in our cells, the Y chromosome, which bears the male sex-determining gene, is passed essentially unchanged from father to son, barring rare mutations.

The researchers extracted DNA from cells scraped from the inner cheeks of 188 unrelated, self-identified Cohanim from Israel, North America, and Britain. They then looked for the presence or absence of a well-studied small stretch of DNA on the Y chromosome called yap, or "Y."

If this hereditary tradition has been closely followed, the Y-chromosomes of the Cohanim today should bear some resemblance to one another because of their unbroken link back to a common ancestor, Aaron.

The "Y" Factor

Genetic studies among Cohanim from all over the world say about 50 percent of Cohanim have that unusual set of genetic markers on their Y chromosome.

What is equally striking is that this genetic signature of the Cohanim is extremely rare outside of Jewish populations.

The Y chromosome also keeps track of time. Small mutations occur in the DNA being passed on, and these changes build up with each generation. Like the tick of a clock, the number of these mutations is a measure of time passed.

By looking at the differences between Y-chromosomes in the Cohanim, researchers can estimate roughly how many generations ago members of the priesthood had a common ancestor.

Remarkably, the evidence suggests the Cohanim chromosomes coalesce at a date that corresponds with the generation of Aaron.

This proves to a scientific certainty that the Jews of Israel are the physical descendants of the Promise.

Currently a group of rabbis is quietly seeking families of the Jewish priestly caste (Cohanim) who are willing to hand over their newborn sons for a special mission: to be raised in conditions of isolation and ritual purity in order to deal with the next red heifer, if and when she is found.

According to the organizers, sons of Cohanim raised in purity, under conditions stipulated by *halacha*, or Jewish law, are essential for the purification of those ritually defiled by the dead. Cohanim who are themselves ritually defiled, as already noted, cannot prepare the red heifer for burning or prepare her ashes for sprinkling on the ritually defiled among the People of Israel.

And the search for a ritually pure red heifer continues. One was believed to have been born in Israel last year, but was subsequently disqualified after it developed a blemish.

The Cohanim Gene proves that the nation "born in a day" on May 14, 1948 is the hereditary nation of Israel whose rebirth Scripture says marks the birth of the generation that will see the return of Christ.

History? Or Future History?

From our perspective on the timeline, the restoration of Israel, and the events leading up to that restoration, are a matter of history.

There is no need to interpret or spiritualize or allegorize the events of Israel's rebirth - there are plenty of personal witnesses besides Abba Eban's.

Israel very nearly became a Soviet client state because of institutionalized anti-Semitism at the highest levels of the US government that threatened to derail recognition of Israel's existence.

The subsequent friendship that developed between the new Jewish state and the United States resulted in a Soviet moratorium on Jewish emigration that lasted until the late 1980's.

And, until the 11th hour, nobody, including the Jews, even knew what the name of the new Jewish state would be.

There are those who would argue that all Bible prophecy was fulfilled by A.D. 70 with the destruction of the Jewish Temple and the dispersion of the Jews.

What appears to be the fulfillment of Bible prophecy in this generation, the argument goes, is the consequence of misreading or misinterpreting the Scriptures.

That argument is belied by recent history, and despite efforts to revise history, there are still too many personal witnesses who were there to see Israel's rebirth as it happened.

The BIG Picture View

You'll recall that the prophet Ezekiel wrote, sometime around the year 536 B.C., that the Jews of the "latter years" would be restored to their original homeland and would be known as the nation of Israel.

One hundred and sixty-six years before, Sargon II of Assyria besieged and divided Israel and Judea, capturing the Kingdom of Israel. Sargon II followed the practice of removing the nobles from a conquered land and settling them elsewhere. As a consequence, the nation of "Israel" ceased to exist and its people became known to history as the *Ten Lost Tribes* of Israel.

When Nebuchadnezzar conquered Judea and settled Judean nobility in Babylon during Ezekiel's lifetime, there was no reason to expect the Jews to escape the same fate as their Israelite cousins 166 years earlier.

But Ezekiel, under Divine inspiration, not only predicted the restoration of a Jewish State, he confidently predicted it would bear the name of a nation that had not existed for generations!

The Last Generation

Even Israel's Founding Fathers, like David Ben-Gurion and Abba Eban didn't know what the new Jewish state would call itself - but Ezekiel knew the answer 2,500 years earlier - and said so, in writing.

The Soviet moratorium against Jewish emigration to the Holy Land meant that most Jewish émigrés came from the Arab states to the east of Israel and those from the Western alliance countries.

Jews from the north (Moscow is due north of Jerusalem) and the Jews from the South (Africa) languished in their host countries, essentially as political prisoners of the Soviet system.

The prophet Isaiah, who lived at about the time of the destruction of the Northern Kingdom, prophesied:

> Fear not: for I am with thee: I will bring thy seed from the east, and gather thee from the west; I will say to the north, Give up; and to the south, Keep not back: bring my sons from far, and my daughters from the ends of the earth;

> (Isaiah 43:4-5)

As noted, we are looking backward to Israel's restoration as history. The Bible's prophets were looking forward, thousands of years into the future.

Looking back, we can see that Israel's "seed from the east" began flocking to the Holy Land following the defeat of the Turkish Ottoman Empire in 1917.

Israel's relationship with the West prompted the mass emigration of Jews from America. The Holocaust spurred a mass emigration of Jews from Western Europe.

It took the dissolution of the Soviet Union and the fall of the Berlin Wall to make the Soviets to the north "give up." Egyptian Jews weren't free to emigrate until after the 1977 Camp David Accords.

And it wasn't until the mid 1990's that places like Ethiopia, and Libya lifted their ban on Jewish emigration. Yemeni Jews were transferred *enmasse*; some 56,000 of them, during what Israel called "Operation Flying Carpet" ("to the south, keep not back").

In the past decade, members of what were believed to be one of the *Lost Tribes* - the tribe of Dan - have turned up in Ethiopia.

Genetic testing has also determined that the men of the African *Lemba* tribe, a black, Bantu-speaking people, share the unique "Y" chromosome of the Cohanim, the Jewish priestly class descended from Aaron.

The *Pathans* of Afghanistan are believed by some to be descended from one of the Lost Tribes.

Chief Rabbi of the Sephardic Jews, Shlomo Amar recently determined that the *Bnei Menashe* community in India's north-east is descended from the *Lost Tribes* and has formally declared them to be Jews. Many have since immigrated to Israel; about 8,000 more are getting ready to do the same.

> And I will make them one nation in the land upon the mountains of Israel; and one king shall be king to them all: and they shall be *no more two nations*, neither shall they be divided into two kingdoms any more at all. [6]
>
> (Ezekiel 37:22)

The Last Generation

It is no Scriptural sleight-of-hand trick, or a manipulation or misinterpretation of the Bible. The restoration of Israel - viewed from our vantage point as personal witnesses to recent history - is an *exact* match to the Bible's description of how, when and where that restoration would take place.

The only difference is that of perspective. To the Bible prophets, it was future, whereas to we who are alive and remain in this generation, it is history past.

> And He spake to them a parable; Behold the fig tree, and all the trees; When they now shoot forth, ye see and know of your own selves that summer is now nigh at hand. So likewise ye, when ye see these things come to pass, know ye that the kingdom of God is nigh at hand. Verily I say unto you, This generation *shall not pass away*, till *all* be fulfilled.[7]

(Luke 21:29-32)

CHAPTER TWO

THE ALIGNMENT OF NATIONS

Where is America In Bible Prophecy?

For skeptics, one of the arguments against the accuracy of the Bible is the apparent absence of any nation resembling the United States represented in the *Big Picture* for the last days.

According to the Bible, the world in the last days is divided into four global spheres of influence. The prophet Daniel identifies a revived form of the Roman Empire, which corresponds to the existing Western European Union.

Daniel prophesied of a revived form of Rome's two legs of iron, represented by the ten toes of iron mixed with clay. Daniel himself interpreted the symbolism of iron and clay, saying the kingdom would be "partly strong and partly weak."

> And whereas thou sawest iron mixed with miry clay, they shall mingle themselves with the seed of men: but they shall not cleave one to another, even as iron is not mixed with clay.
>
> (Daniel 2:43)

The Bible predicts the rise of three other spheres of global power, identified variously as the "Gog-Magog Alliance," the "Kings of the East" and the "Kings of the South."

Currently, five global spheres of power exist in the world. The four mentioned above are in a state of flux; realigning themselves, almost against reason, to conform to the scenario outlined by Scripture.

The fifth, the United States, grows increasingly isolated. Washington is so lonely it has gone into denial, embracing any nation as an important ally that isn't openly at war with it.

Prime examples of America's *pretend* friends include Saudi Arabia, Kuwait, Pakistan and the core group of Western European nations led by France and Germany. They are our *friends* in the sense they are not currently enemies.

America has only one unquestioning and unequivocal ally within the sea of nations. That ally, the land of Israel, is the central character around which the entire end-time drama is played out.

There is no mention of a fifth, overarching global superpower resembling the United States. For years, well-meaning Christians have tried to find some reference to America in Bible prophecy.

In this chapter, we'll examine the developing global political alliances of the early 21st century and compare them, side by side with the prophecies of Scripture for the last days, and see if we can discover the answer to the question, "Where is America in Bible Prophecy?"

Ezekiel's Gog

According to the prophet Ezekiel, there will arise in the last days, a massive military and political alliance more-or-less formally known as the "Gog-Magog Alliance."

"Son of man, set thy face against Gog, the land of Magog, the chief prince of Meshech and Tubal, and prophesy against him…" (Ezekiel 38:2).

According to Ezekiel, Gog and Magog will lead an alliance of nations in the last days in a disastrous (for them) invasion against the reborn nation of Israel.

Ezekiel clearly identifies Gog as a person, rather than a place; "the prince of Meshech and Tubal."

The Scofield Reference Bible's notes to Ezekiel claim that "Meshech" is a Hebrew form of Moscow, and that "Tubal" represents the Siberian capital Tobolsk.

That interpretation would make Gog both a *place* - the Russian Federation of Nations - and a *person* - in the sense of a federated Russian leadership.

The Interlinear Bible (Hebrew/Greek/English) renders that verse as: "Son of man, set your face toward Gog, the land of Magog, the prince of Rosh, Meshech, and Tubal; and prophesy concerning him" (In Hebrew, the word *Rosh* means, *chief prince*, or, the *chief of the chief princes*).

Magog was a son of Japheth, who, together with his brothers Tubal, Meshech, and Togarmah (Genesis 10:2-3) settled what are modern-day Russia and the southern steppes of the Caucasus Mountains.

Ezekiel identifies *Gog* as coming from the north of Israel. Following the compass due north from Jerusalem will take you through the center of Moscow.

The army of Gog and Magog primarily includes people from the nations of Gog, Gomer, Tubal, Meshech, and the house of Togarmah from the "north parts." They will be joined by Persia from the east, Put from the west, Cush from the south, and others.

> Persia, Ethiopia, and Libya with them; all of them with shield and helmet: Gomer, and all his bands; the house of Togarmah of the north quarters, and all his bands: and many people with thee....

(Ezekiel 38:5-6)

"Gomer" is mentioned in Genesis as well as Ezekiel. The Jewish-turned-Roman historian Flavius Josephus identified Gomer with the Galatians.

"For Gomer founded those whom the Greeks now call Galatians, (Galls) but were then called Gomerites."[1]

Ancient Galatia was an area in the highlands of central Anatolia (now Turkey). Galatia was bounded on the north by Bithynia and Paphlagonia, on the east by Pontus, on the south by Lycaonia and Cappadocia, and on the west by the remainder of Phrygia, the eastern part of which the Gauls had invaded.

A Tale of Two Turkeys

The modern capital of Turkey, Ankara, is part of ancient Galatia. Turkey is among the most Westernized and prosperous states of the Islamic world, which, in itself is fascinating, since, until 1917, Turkey *was* the Islamic world.

The sultans of the Ottoman Empire ruled from what is modern-day Turkey for four hundred years before siding with Kaiser Wilhelm II of Germany in the First World War This fatal error in judgment on the part of Sultan of Turkey, Abdul Hamid II, resulted in the breakup of the Ottoman Empire into the modern states of the Middle East.

Before we move on, let's consider the historical reasons for the Ottoman's alliance with the Kaiser in 1914. A series of military defeats in the 19th century had compelled the Turks to grant zones of influence to European powers: Egypt to Britain; Syria and the Lebanon to France; Bosnia-Herzegovina to Austria-Hungary; and Libya to Italy.

The Ottoman's main objective in war was the same then as the Islamic terror network's objective in war today - the recovery of "Dar al Islam" (*Zone of Islam*) from the infidels.

Islam divides the world into two zones; the Zone of Islam, (which includes any and all territory that was ever subject to Islamic rule, including Jerusalem) and the "Dar al Harb" (*Zone of War*). The ultimate objective of Islam (Islam means literally "submission") is in two stages: the first is to recover all of "Dar al Islam"; the second is to spread Islam to the "Dar al Harb."

In other words, according to Islam, only two zones exist in the world; that under the *submission* of Islam, and that of war to bring under the *submission* of Islam.

Turkey is the historical heart and soul of Islam's former greatness. It ruled an Islamic Empire for four hundred years until its defeat and subsequent breakup by the victorious Allied forces in World War One.

White Meat or Dark?

The Republic of Turkey was founded in 1923 as a constitutionally-mandated secular state. Its constitution expressly empowers the Turkish military with the responsibility of national unity. The army therefore plays a formal political role as guardian of the secular, unified nature of the republic.

The Last Generation

In a 2002 electoral upset, Turkish voters gave the Islamic *AKP* ("Justice and Development Party") an absolute parliamentary majority. The *AKP* is the successor to the Islamic *Welfare Party*, which briefly led a coalition government before being broken up in 2000 by the army as a threat to Turkey's secular government.

In 2002, in the face of such a strong voter mandate, the Turkish army, though wary, acquiesced to Islamic influence, if not full Islamic authority in the governing of Turkish affairs.

Turkey is the only Islamic state to be a full member of NATO. Currently, the Turks are stumping for membership in the European Union. France and Germany are trying to freeze them out. This leaves Islamic Turkey surrounded by Islamic former provinces of the Islamic Ottoman Empire itching for a confrontation with both Israel and the West.

Ottoman Lite?

Among the nations listed by Ezekiel as participants in the last days Gog-Magog war against Israel is a nation called "Togarmah." Overlaid on a modern map, what emerges is a sort of "Ottoman Lite."

Ezekiel 38: 6 adds "Gomer" and "Beth-Togarmah" to the Gog-Magog coalition. Gomer was the first son of Japheth. The Gomerites were the ancient Cimmerians, expelled in 700 B.C. from the southern steppes of Russia into what today is Turkey.

Historically, "Gomer" is also linked to the ancient Cimmerians. The Cimmerians eventually settled the regions north of the Caucasus and the Black Sea, in what is now parts of Russia and the Ukraine.

The Cimmerians are believed to have migrated north from the region now called Azerbaijan around the time of Nebuchadnezzar of Babylon. Both the ancient Cimmerians and the Gomerites spoke a form of the Thracian or Persian language.

"Togarmah" was the third son of Gomer and *Beth* at the beginning of the name is the Hebrew word for "house" or "place of." In Ezekiel's time there was a city in Cappodocia (Modern Turkey) known as *Tegarma, Tagarma, Til-garimmu,* or *Takarama.*

Ironically, it appears that German and French opposition to Turkey's admission into the Union may drive the Turks away from the West and deeper into the Islamic world. Politically, a lot can happen in a very short time.

It is important to remember that until 1979, Iran, like Turkey, was a close ally of the United States, and one of the most heavily Westernized nations in the Islamic world. Then the Shah was deposed, the Ayatollahs came to power. Iran quickly became the West's worst nightmare.

In the mid-1970's, prophecy scholars were scratching their heads over Persia's inclusion in the Gog-Magog roster; just like Turkey, it didn't seem to make any sense.

How could modern Iran, with its secular government and strong ties to the West, find itself part of a Russian-led invasion of Israel? By 1980, it was pretty obvious. Amazing what can happen in a few years.

Remember, it was almost 2,600 years ago that Ezekiel confidently penned the exact roster of nations that would move against Israel in the last days!

Less than thirty years ago Iran was our friend. Today, it is a Russian nuclear client state with ties to al-Qaeda and

Hezbollah, and is dedicated to the destruction of both the United States and Israel.

Today, Turkey is moving in the same direction - away from the West and back into the traditional Islamic world.

It is worth remembering that Turkey, although a NATO member, blindsided the US administration by refusing to allow its territory as a staging point for US forces, causing coalition military planners to rewrite their plans for the invasion of Iraq; clearly a show of Islamic solidarity.

Another membership rejection from the EU could be enough to push Turkey all the way over to *Dar al Islam*, precisely as Ezekiel predicted.

Not long ago, Russia was the Soviet Union and Iran was America's closest ally, with Turkey running a close second. Most Americans had never heard of Islam, and even if they had, the phrase, "radical Islam" had not yet entered the American lexicon.

Ezekiel's roster is almost complete.

And Many Bands with Thee

Tubal was another son of Japheth who settled the area. Josephus wrote: "Tobal gave rise to the Thobeles, who are now called Iberes." Josephus' "Iberes" settled in the area of the former Soviet state of Georgia.

Ezekiel begins his listing of Gog-Magog's allies with Persia, or modern day Iran. Iran's allies, according to Ezekiel, include Ethiopia and Libya.

The Libya of Ezekiel's day wasn't Muammar Ghadaffi's Libya. Josephus writes: "Phut also was the founder of Libya to the south and called the inhabitants Phutites, from himself" (some Bible translations render "Libya" [KJV], others render "Put" - a grandson of Noah).

Put settled an area that included most of North Africa including Libya and parts of modern Egypt.

"Ethiopia" (rendered in some versions as "Cush") was a civilization centered in the North African region of Nubia, located in what is today southern Egypt and northern Sudan.

Cush was the father of Nimrod. Josephus gives an account of the nation of Cush (*Chus*), who is the son of Ham and the grandson of Noah.

> For of the four sons of Ham, time has not at all hurt the name of Chus; for the Ethiopians, over whom he reigned, are even at this day, both by themselves and by all men in Asia, called Chusites.[2]

In the 5th century A.D. the Himyarites, in the south of Arabia, were styled by Syrian writers as Cushaeans and Ethiopians, and it is certain that the present-day areas of Yemen and Eritrea were ruled together by one dynasty at that time.

The African "Kush" covered Upper Egypt, and extended southwards from the First Cataract. In addition, the Cushitic peoples, who live around the Horn of Africa today, comprising the Somali, Afar, Oromo and several other tribes, are popularly asserted to be the offspring of the Biblical Cush.

That the Biblical term was also applied to parts of Arabia, where Cush is the eponymous father of certain tribal and ethnic designations.

Babylonian inscriptions mention the *Kashshi* or *Kassites*; it was once held that this signified a possible explanation of Cush, the ancestor of Nimrod in Genesis chapter 8.

The rhetorical question, "Can the Cushite change his skin?" in Jeremiah 13:23 implies people of a notably different skin color from the Israelites; most probably an African race.

The Septuagint Greek translation of the Old Testament uniformly translates Cush as "Ethiopia."

What We Know So Far

So, this is what we know. We know that Ezekiel predicts that, "in the latter days" the chief of chief princes of an alliance called Gog-Magog will arise from a location to the uttermost north of Israel.

We know that due north of Jerusalem on the same longitude is the modern city of Moscow.

We know that Gog will be reluctantly drawn into a conflict with Israel. Ezekiel says Gog will be *drawn* into this conflict, as if he had *hooks in his jaws*.

The Gog-Magog alliance includes modern Russia, the Ukraine, Iran, Iraq, Turkey, North Africa, and the Middle East extending from the Mediterranean Sea to the Persian Gulf.

We also know that the target of the Gog Magog Alliance is the restored nation of Israel. And finally, we know the time frame. Ezekiel says it will take place "in the latter days." Here is something else we know. Ezekiel's alignment of nations was never possible in previous generations.

To begin with, Ezekiel's scenario demands the existence of Israel:

> ...the land that is brought back from the sword, and is gathered out of many people, against the mountains of Israel, which have been always waste: but it is brought forth out of the nations....
>
> (Ezekiel 38:8-9)

From Ezekiel's day until May 14, 1948, there was no place on earth called "Israel." Prior to 1948, Russia had little interest in the Middle East. The Middle East had been part of the Islamic Ottoman Empire since the time of Columbus.

Ezekiel lived one thousand years before Mohammed introduced Islam to the world and twenty-five hundred years before David Ben-Gurion announced the rebirth of Israel on May 14, 1948.

The fulfillment of Ezekiel's Gog-Magog prophecy depends entirely on the simultaneous development of two events; the rebirth of Israel and the rebirth of Mohammedan-style radical Islam.

What Comes Next?

Look at Ezekiel's main antagonists. There are three.

The first is Gog and Magog, the modern Russian federation. Gog and Magog's participation in the invasion force, according to Ezekiel, comes as a result of God's promise to "turn thee back, and put hooks into thy jaws, and I will bring thee forth..." (Ezekiel 38:4).

I've often pondered the phrase, "turn thee back" (Hebrew "paqad," literally "call to remembrance"). I recall writing a piece for *This Week in Bible Prophecy* in 1992. The story was about the new Russian parliament suddenly breaking mid-session to rush out to the halls of the Duma where newly-admitted Western missionaries were handing out free New Testaments.

Having just emerged from a lifetime of godless Communism, Russians were eager to hear the Word of God and Christian missionaries were welcomed with open arms.

For several years, Russians were offered this "call to remembrance" of Scripture before former KGB operative Vladimir Putin slammed the door shut on foreign missionaries. The Russian Orthodox Church - which was heavily infiltrated by the KGB during the Communist era – was to be the only recognized Christian religion in Russia.

The "call to remembrance" was over. When Moscow later entered into its nuclear agreement with Iran, the hook was set.

The second of Ezekiel's antagonists is the alliance itself.

Look at the list carefully. Every nation and region named as Gog-Magog allies is part of the Islamic world - every single one of them.

Islamic North Africa, (Ethiopia and Libya) including the Sudan, whose government is currently conducted genocide against its Christian population.

Saudi Arabia, the birthplace of Islam and the heart and soul of radical Wahabbist jihadist Islam.

Turkey (ruled by the Islamic Party), together with most of the Russian Republic's Islamic *stans*.

The Iranian Connection

Persia, or modern Iran, could well be the "hook in Gog's jaw." Iran's nuclear program was built by, overseen, guarded and maintained by Russian scientists, technicians and military forces; all of whom would become victims of a hostile air strike against Iran's nuclear facilities.

Iran's leader, Mahmoud Ahmadinejad, has made it something of a habit to mention the destruction of Israel in every speech.

Iran was known as "Persia" until the early 1920's when the country's name was changed to Iran. The other nations on Ezekiel's roster are all either Russian client states or old Soviet client states, with the exception of Turkey - which is rapidly being pushed back into the Islamic world by the European Union.

> After many days thou shalt be visited: in the latter years thou shalt come into the land that is brought back from the sword, and is gathered out of many people, against the mountains of Israel, which have been always waste: but it is brought forth out of the nations, and they shall dwell safely all of them.
>
> (Ezekiel 38: 8)

We learn much from this one passage. We learn that the war is slated to take place in the "latter years" - once Israel had resumed her place at the table of nations. The entire history of the Israeli Diaspora is contained in this one verse.

In Ezekiel's day, "Israel" had not existed for generations and the Kingdom of Judah was in Babylonian hands. From 702 B.C. until 1948, there was no place on earth called *Israel*. Israel was "gathered out of many people" the land was "brought back from the sword" (it took five wars, including a War of Independence to do it).

Until the Jews returned to the Land, it had "always been waste" exactly as Ezekiel predicted, but now that it is "brought forth out of the nations," the Jews again have a homeland where they can take refuge from persecution.

Ezekiel's prophecy is like a jigsaw puzzle. The more pieces that fall into place, the clearer the final picture becomes. Iran's nuclear plans cannot be permitted to come to fruition. Include those pieces and the picture that emerges looks amazingly like the one painted by Ezekiel, from exile in Babylon twenty-five hundred years ago.

The King of the South

> And at the time of the end shall the king of the south push at him: and the king of the north shall come against him like a whirlwind, with chariots, and with horsemen, and with many ships; and he shall enter into the countries, and shall overflow and pass over.
>
> He shall enter also into the glorious land, and many countries shall be overthrown: but these shall escape out of his hand, even Edom, and Moab, and the chief of the children of Ammon.
>
> He shall stretch forth his hand also upon the countries: and the land of Egypt shall not escape.
>
> But he shall have power over the treasures of gold and of silver, and over all the precious things of Egypt: and the Libyans and the Ethiopians shall be at his steps.
>
> But tidings out of the east and out of the north shall trouble him: therefore he shall go forth with great fury to destroy, and utterly to make away many.
>
> And he shall plant the tabernacles of his palace

between the seas in the glorious holy mountain; yet he
shall come to his end, and none shall help him."

(Daniel 11:40-45)

There are probably as many theories regarding the exact
identity of the King of the South as there are students of
the Book of Daniel. But Daniel gives us a pretty clear
outline of his "kingdom," his conquests, and his eventual
destiny.

His conquests extend into the "glorious land" - a reference
to Israel's territory under the Covenant. "Edom," "Moab"
and "the children of "Ammon" include territory extending
from Israel's West Bank to Amman, the capital of modern
Jordan; from North Africa to Egypt and beyond to
encompass what makes up the modern Arab world.

A Royal Clue

Daniel offers a number of clues regarding the identity of
the "King of the South," his nature and some key
identifying characteristics.

And the king shall do according to his will; and he
shall exalt himself, and magnify himself above every
god, and shall speak marvelous things against the God
of gods, and shall prosper till the indignation be
accomplished: for that that is determined shall be
done.

(Daniel 11:36)

Many students of Daniel identify the king of Daniel 11:36
with the historical Antiochus IV Epiphanes, whose sack of
Jerusalem in 163 B.C. led to the Maccabean Revolt.

Antiochus defiled the Temple by sacrificing a pig in the
Holy of Holies as a direct insult to the God of Israel.

Jesus was recalling Antiochus when He spoke of a coming "abomination of desolation" to take place during the Tribulation Period.

> When ye therefore shall see the abomination of desolation, spoken of by Daniel the prophet, stand in the holy place, (whoso readeth, let him understand:)
>
> (Matthew 24:15)

But Jesus included language that suggests His reference back to Daniel was also a clue directed forward to the generation that would see the fulfillment of His Words.

Once the holy place was defiled by the presence of an unclean animal, it became religiously desolate until it could be ritually purified. Ritual purification of the Holy of Holies required ritually pure priests following defined religious rules using ritually required Temple instruments.

Jesus warned of a religious abomination that would "stand in the holy place" that would cause a religious desolation as utter and complete as was effected by Antiochus IV Epiphanes.

The al-Aqsa Mosque has stood on the site of the holy place since its construction by Caliph 'Abd al-Malik at the end of the seventh century A.D.. The existence of a religious shrine to Allah is an abomination to Judaism that has so completely desecrated the Temple Mount that religious Jews who set foot on it are ritually defiled.

Daniel says that, having exalted himself above every god ("There is no god but Allah") and speaking against the God of gods, he shall "prosper until the indignation be accomplished" - i.e. the elimination of the abomination standing in the holy place.

It is no accident that the bulk of the Middle Eastern oil supply is located in the Islamic world. Rather, it is a fulfillment of Daniel's prophecy.

Daniel also predicts that prosperity will be abruptly revoked. Since the majority of the Islamic Middle East is totally dependent on oil revenues, all it would take is the development of an alternative to oil to bring their economies to a grinding halt.

Daniel gives other clues about the King of the South.

"Neither shall he regard the God of his fathers, nor the desire of women, nor regard any god: for he shall magnify himself above all" (Daniel 11:37).

Concerning "regarding other gods," although Islam traces its lineage back to Abraham and claims kinship with Christians and Jews as "People of the Book" it rejects the Old and New Testament records as hopelessly corrupted, rejects the Abrahamic Covenant with Isaac and his descendants, and denies the deity of Jesus Christ.

Islam regards a woman as worth only half as much as a man, permits wife-beating as an Islamic "right of marriage," rejects women's suffrage, permits honor killings, opposes education for women and generally disregards the desire of women as a matter of religious doctrine.

Although Islamic apologists claim Islam to be tolerant of other religions (other gods) non-Muslims in Islamic countries are regarded as "dhimmis" – second class citizens, with virtually no civil rights and subject to a special tax called a "jizya." A *dhimmi's* life is valued at one half that of a Muslim. The maximum punishment for murdering a *dhimmi* is payment of blood money. No death penalty is possible.

Dhimmis are not allowed to carry weapons. They have no right of self-defense against a Muslim. Their testimony is not permitted in Muslim courts. A *dhimmi* cannot inherit from a Muslim. And Islamic law permits the enslavement of free *dhimmis* living in Islamic lands.

During the reign of the Islamic Taliban in Afghanistan, they shocked the world by blowing up a fifteen-hundred year old Buddhist monument that it claimed was an offense to Allah.

One of Islam's Pillars of Faith dictates that "there is no god but Allah and Mohammed is his prophet." If Islam has a king, it is Mohammed.

> Thus shall he do in the most strong holds with a strange god, whom he shall acknowledge and increase with glory: and he shall cause them to rule over many, and shall divide the land for gain.

> (Daniel 11:39)

Islam's record of conquest over the centuries is impressive. Discussed earlier, territory once ceded or conquered becomes part of Dar al Islam. In the view of Islam, it remains a permanent Islamic possession, to the glory of Allah. The entire Middle East Peace Process is constructed upon the misguided Western policy of "land for peace" - dividing the land (of Israel) between the Jews and Arabs in order to gain peace.

The Kings of the East

The Apostle John refers to a vast army from the east that will exist as a fourth sphere of global influence in the last days. Unlike the unified King of the South, John describes a multinational force arising from east of the Euphrates River.

And the sixth angel poured out his vial upon the great river Euphrates; and the water thereof was dried up, that the way of the kings of the east might be prepared.

(Revelation 16:12)

John doesn't give many specifics regarding the ethnicity of the eastern alliance, but one detail he does provide is particularly revealing.

"Saying to the sixth angel which had the trumpet, Loose the four angels which are bound in the great river Euphrates" (Revelation 9:15).

It is the sixth angel that dries up the Euphrates, making the way for the kings of the east in Revelation 16 and the sixth angel who looses the four angels that lead the Oriental army.

Here's the clue: "And the number of the army of the horsemen were two hundred thousand thousand: and I heard the number of them" (Revelation 9:16).

Two hundred thousand thousand – an army of two hundred million men! Such a number must have sounded preposterous to the Apostle John. There weren't that many men of military age on earth in his day. An army that big would leave no one left to fight.

But to the generation to whom end time prophecy would be relevant, it makes perfect sense. _The CIA World Factbook_ estimates that China's military reserves, including able-bodied men fit for military service, numbers two hundred and eighty-one million - and that's just the men!

China is the nuclear Big Dragon of the _Dragon Nations of ASEAN_, which consists of the ten "Little Dragon Nations" of the Orient: Cambodia, Indonesia, Laos, Malaysia, Myanmar, the Philippines, Singapore, Thailand, Vietnam and Brunei. China is the patron/protector of the crazy, nuclear-armed dictatorship of North Korea, and is perceived by many analysts as destined to become America's chief competitor and rival as the 21st century progresses.

> And thus I saw the horses in the vision, and them that sat on them, having breastplates of fire, and of jacinth, and brimstone: and the heads of the horses were as the heads of lions; and out of their mouths issued fire and smoke and brimstone. By these three was the third part of men killed, by the *fire*, and by the *smoke*, and by the *brimstone*, which issued out of their mouths.
>
> (Revelation 9:17-18)

For two millennia, the faithful scratched their heads and wondered "what the heck does *that* mean?" John was attempting to describe what he saw using the vocabulary available to him in the first century.

Even given the vocabulary limits John was working with, from our vantage point in time and space, we see an unmistakable description of nuclear war.

The North Korean problem won't go away by itself, and China has the most to lose if it isn't made to go away somehow.

I don't claim to have some secret knowledge of the future apart from reading the same Bible you have. But the focus is on that fourth sphere of global influence, the threat is that posed by fire, smoke and brimstone; the likely outcome will be a sea change in the political face of the region.

One possible scenario is a unified Korea, but the drain absorbing the North would put on South Korea, the world's sixth-largest economy, would be crippling. The natural ally of a unified Korea would be China, not Washington. America would no longer serve any purpose in maintaining troops on the Korean peninsula.

It logically follows that Japan would look increasingly toward economic and military alliances in Asia and Western influence would decline - which follows the Bible's scenario of four distinct and separate spheres of global power in the last days.

Gog-Magog (Russia, Iran and allies), the Kings of the South (the surviving Islamic world), the revived Roman Empire and the Kings of the East. No mention of a fifth superpower resembling America. Where did it go?

The Merchants of Tarshish?

For years, well-meaning Christians have tried to find some reference to America in Bible prophecy. The most convincing argument I've heard to date is Ezekiel's reference to the "merchants of Tarshish and all the young lions thereof" (Ezekiel 38:13).

"Tarshish" is a Sanskrit or Aryan word meaning "sea coast." The identity of "merchants of Tarshish" is a subject of wide debate. Some scholars put *Tarshish* on the European coastline to the extreme west; others put it on the coast of India to the east.

But to find America in *Tarshish*, one needs to locate it on Europe's west coast; preferably in Great Britain. The "lion" then represents Britain, and "all the young lions thereof" can include America, a former British colony.

Although the *America as Tarshish Theory* has many champions, you may be able to tell that I am skeptical of this interpretation.

Let's quickly review: During the Tribulation, we find references to Russia and the modern Middle East in Ezekiel's Gog Magog vision. We find references to a massive Oriental power, called the Kings of the East, capable of fielding an army of two hundred million men.

There are references to a pan-African alliance resembling the Organization of African States, and a huge segment of prophecy is devoted exclusively to the revival of the Roman Empire and the role it plays in advancing the antichrist's agenda.

But there is *no* reference to anything resembling a fifth political power, especially not one as powerful alone as are the other four powers combined.

Looking on the Wrong Side

That is not to say there is no mention of America in the Bible for the last days - just not during the Tribulation. We're looking on the wrong side. Let me explain.

One could argue that America represents the Church in the last days, just as the nation of Israel represents Judaism.

If Israel has an indelible identity in the eyes of the world, it is as "the Jewish State." If America's identity can be encapsulated in the world's eyes, it is as the world's most Christian nation; which is why Islam declared war on America in the first place.

To al-Qaeda, the war is against Christians and Jews, and therefore, by definition, it is primarily against America and Israel.

The Apostle Paul's ministry was to the Gentile Church. Although himself a former Pharisee, he was chosen as the "Apostle to the Gentiles." Paul says little about the

Tribulation, but he wrote extensively about the events of the final hours of the Church Age leading up to it.

His description of the moral state of the Church in the last days as recorded in II Timothy 3:1-6 is a letter-perfect description of American society in the 21st century. Paul begins by setting the time frame:

"This know also, that in the last days perilous times shall come."

For America, times have *never* been more perilous. Not even during the darkest days of World War II was the American homeland under direct threat. America had more friends and international prestige in the 1940's while engaged in a war with half the world than it did as it entered the 21st century.

Modern America's social fabric is coming apart at the seams before our very eyes: "men shall be lovers of their own selves, covetous, boasters, proud, blasphemers, disobedient to parents, unthankful, unholy..." (II Timothy 3: 2).

That pretty much sums up the nation's political headlines in the morning newspapers.

> Without natural affection, trucebreakers, false accusers, incontinent, fierce, despisers of those that are good, traitors, heady, highminded, lovers of pleasures more than lovers of God....
>
> (II Timothy 3: 2)

Parents killing kids, teachers raping students, American politicians telling the world America can't be trusted, Christ's banishment from *Christ*mas, the politics of personal destruction replacing the politics of ideas, etc..

Paul's outline couldn't be *more* descriptive of 21st century America. Could it?

The American Civil Liberties Union has made a century-long career out of "defending" civil rights by opposing national recognition of God as the Guarantor of our civil rights. They defend America's God-given civil liberties by mythologizing the God that gives them.

"Having a form of godliness, but denying the power thereof, from such turn away" (II Timothy 3:1-5).

Why America is so clearly envisioned by Paul in the final hours of the Church Age, but so completely absent from the Tribulation record is a subject of considerable debate.

Bible critics argue that America isn't in the record because America didn't exist when the Bible was written. In this view, America's absence is evidence the Bible is really a book written by men and not inspired by an all-knowing God.

II Timothy 3:1-5 mirrors 21st century America so precisely that it demolishes this argument without further comment.

But Where Does America Go?

What would happen to America if suddenly, millions of Americans (including much of the administration, a good chunk of the Pentagon's military leadership and most of the US military) suddenly vanished without a trace?

Behold, I shew you a mystery; We shall not all sleep, but we shall all be changed, In a moment, in the twinkling of an eye, at the last trump: for the trumpet shall sound, and the dead shall be raised incorruptible, and we shall be changed.

(I Corinthians 15:51-52)

So far, we've examined a lot (but not all) of the Bible's track record pertaining to its prophecies of the last days and the signs pointing to the Second Coming of Jesus Christ. It would take more faith that I could muster to believe it is all coincidental.

The Bible also predicts that, before the onset of the Great Tribulation, the Lord will remove the believing Church in accordance with His promise:

> In My Father's house are many mansions: if it were not so, I would have told you. I go to prepare a place for you. And if I go and prepare a place for you, I will come again, and *receive you unto Myself;* that where I am, there ye may be also.[3]

(John 14:2-3)

The Apostle Paul describes the event in greater detail in his first Epistle to the Thessalonians:

> For the Lord Himself shall descend from heaven with a shout, with the voice of the archangel, and with the trump of God: and the dead in Christ shall rise first: Then we which are alive and remain shall be caught up together with them in the clouds, to meet the Lord in the air: and so shall we ever be with the Lord.

(I Thessalonians 4:16-17)

I can almost hear some of you now: "Whoa, Jack! I was okay with all the rest of this stuff, but are you saying what I think you are saying? Christians are going to be taken, bodily and still alive, directly to Heaven?"

Before you close this book, consider what we've learned of the accuracy of Bible prophecy so far and bear with me a bit longer.

Daniel's Seventy Weeks

What is the purpose of the Tribulation period? The answer should go a long way toward helping us to understand whether or not the Church will be raptured before the Tribulation Period, out of it, or after it.

We begin with the Prophet Daniel. Daniel was given a vision of history as it would unfold. Daniel foretold the rise and fall of three great empires and the rise, fall and revival of the last great world empire - that of Rome.

Daniel was given a complete outline of Israel's future history, broken into subdivisions of time of seven years each. In Hebrew, "shabua," translated as "week" in Daniel 9:24, is a *week of years*, in much the same way the Greek system is in use today. A "decade" denotes ten years in the way a "shabua" or "week" denotes seven years.

> Seventy weeks are determined upon thy people and upon thy holy city, to finish the transgression, and to make an end of sins, and to make reconciliation for iniquity, and to bring in everlasting righteousness, and to seal up the vision and prophecy, and to anoint the most Holy.
>
> Daniel 9:24

In this verse, we see a six-fold purpose to be accomplished in Daniel's "Seventy Weeks" or 490 years. First, to finish Israel's sin – the rejection of the Messiah at the First Advent. Then there is a skip forward in time to His Second Advent, at which time, an end will be made of sin and reconciliation will be made for Israel's iniquity.

Everlasting righteousness will be introduced to Israel. Scriptures will be vindicated by the fulfillment of all prophecy. And finally, the return of Christ at the conclusion of the war of Armageddon, at which time He will be anointed and will take His seat at the Throne of David.

Daniel's angel went on to lock in the time.

> Know therefore and understand, that from the going forth of the commandment to restore and to build Jerusalem unto the Messiah the Prince shall be seven weeks, and threescore and two weeks ... And after threescore and two weeks shall Messiah be cut off, but not for himself:
>
> (Daniel 9:25, 26)

Beginning at a specific point in history and moving forward in time, the angel said that after sixty-nine weeks, or 483 years, the Messiah shall be cut off (killed) but not for Himself (He was blameless).

History records only one decree that authorized the rebuilding of the city.

> And it came to pass in the month Nisan, in the twentieth year of Artaxerxes the king... I said unto the king, If it please the king, and if thy servant have found favour in thy sight, that thou wouldest send me unto Judah, unto the city of my fathers' sepulchres, that I may build it.
>
> (Nehemiah 2:1, 5)

According to modern dating research, the 20th year of the Persian king Xerxes would have been 444 B.C. The reference to the "month of Nisan" with no reference to the day indicates the first day of the month. Using the Hebrew calendar, the first day of Nisan, 444 B.C. corresponds to the modern date of March 5.

Counting forward from 444 B.C. to A.D. 33 is 477 years. But 1 B.C. and A.D. 1 are the same year, so deducting that year leaves us with 476 years. 476 years times 365.24219879 days (per year) equals 173,855 days. Jesus was crucified on March 30, A.D. 33, so there are an extra twenty-five days to add to the equation, giving a grand total of 173,880 days.[4]

So, from the going forth of the commandment on March 5, 444 B.C. until March 30, A.D. 33 was exactly 173,880 days divided by 360 day lunar calendar equals exactly 483 years. Daniel 9:26 goes on to say that after Messiah is "cut off, but not for himself ... the people of the prince that shall come shall destroy the city...."

Within a generation of Israel's rejection of the Messiah, General (and future Emperor) Titus of Rome led his legions into Jerusalem where the city was sacked and the Temple utterly destroyed.

The *people* identified by the angel to Daniel are proved by history to be the Roman Empire, currently embodied by the European Union. The *prince* of that *people* is the antichrist.

According to the Jewish historian (and eyewitness) Josephus, the Romans burned the Temple so completely its ornate gold fixtures melted and ran between the stones of the Temple.

To recover this rich booty, the soldiers dismantled the Temple, stone by stone, fulfilling Jesus' prophecy of a generation before; "There shall not be left here one stone upon another, that shall not be thrown down" (Matthew 24:2).

The coming prince of Daniel 9:26, the antichrist, kicks off the Tribulation Period - and starts the clock running - with an event as historically definite as was Artexerxe's Decree.

According to Daniel 9:27, the antichrist "confirms a covenant" between Israel and her enemies. This "covenant," or treaty, is confirmed as an agreement of seven year's duration (Not coincidentally, the exact length of the Tribulation Period - Daniel's Seventieth Week).

The Book of Daniel prophesies that from the signing of that treaty until it is broken by the antichrist is three and one-half years ("time, times and a half"). As further confirmation, the time period between the breaking of the treaty at the midpoint until the return of Christ is precisely 1260 days - three and one-half years.

We have already seen the precision with which God counted down sixty-nine weeks of years. One week remains. There is no reason to think God has fired His accountant.

It follows that, anyone familiar with the Scriptures who observes the breaking of the treaty with Israel by antichrist, could know exactly, to the day, when Jesus was prophesied to return.

But wait! What about what Jesus Himself said of His coming? He said, "But of that day and hour knoweth no man, no, not the angels of heaven, but my Father only" (Matthew 24:36).

Clearly, He could not have been speaking of the same event; one that could be so easily calculated. Is this a contradiction?

The Rapture

According to I Thessalonians Chapter 4, there is a secret return of Christ for His Church before the Tribulation Period can proceed.

Paul writes:

> For this we say unto you by the word of the Lord, that
> we which are alive and remain unto the coming of the
> Lord shall not prevent (precede) them which are
> asleep. For the Lord himself shall descend from
> heaven with a shout, with the voice of the archangel,
> and with the trump of God: and the dead in Christ shall
> rise first: Then we which are alive and remain shall be
> caught up together with them in the clouds, to meet the
> Lord in the air: and so shall we ever be with the Lord.

This secret Advent, in which the Lord comes for His
Church in the air, is not the same event as the one in which
He puts His foot upon the Mount of Olives, splitting it in
two (Zechariah 14:4). Paul's description of the Lord's
coming has Him coming in the air, not touching down to
earth.

Paul is referring to what is commonly called the Rapture of
the Church. Since this secret Advent's timing cannot,
according to Jesus, be calculated, it cannot be the same
event as the Second Coming. That Triumphant Return can
be calculated precisely; one minute after the antichrist
signs the seven year treaty.

Since the Tribulation Period is the time of "Jacob's
Trouble" - Daniel's Seventieth Week, it is a time reserved
for Israel, not the Church. Remember, it is to make
"reconciliation for sin" and to "bring in everlasting
righteousness."

For the Church during the Church Age, those goals were
already accomplished at the Cross.

But the Tribulation Period is the final week of the Age of
the Law. The Temple will be in full operation and the

Mosaic Law in full force. The Church Age is concluded with the antichrist's treaty.

Given the current situation in the Middle East, some kind of confirmation of a seven year agreement (like Oslo) is an absolute necessity, either to prevent all out war or at the conclusion of any such war.

Bible prophecy says it will happen. The Bible also says it begins a time of judgment against Israel and the Gentile world. The Church was already judged at the Cross.

Here's what it all means, boiled down into a single sentence: *At some point before that treaty is signed, Jesus Christ will descend from heaven with a shout, and the voice of an archangel, and all those living who placed their faith in Christ will be snatched away, to be forever with Christ.*

That treaty could happen at almost any moment. And that means the Rapture of the Church is even closer.

A Great Escape?

One of the principle misunderstandings concerning the Rapture revolves around its purpose. Critics of a pre-tribulation rapture deride it as some pie-in-the-sky "Great Escape" for Christians living in the last days.

There is no such promise of "escape" from tribulation, they argue, and (correctly) point out the Bible's promise that "in this world ye shall have tribulation" so the pre-tribulational hope of a "Great Escape" is not only delusional, it is unscriptural.

In fact, if the pre-tribulational hope *was* for a "Great Escape" from tribulation, the critics would be correct. There is *no* promise that the Church will escape tribulation, but there is an iron-clad promise that the Church will not go through the seven years of tribulation described by Jeremiah as the "Time of Jacob's Trouble" and outlined by Daniel as Israel's "Seventieth Week."

There are several reasons for a pre-tribulational Rapture, not the least of which is the purpose of the Tribulation in God's unfolding plan for the ages.

The purpose of the seven year Tribulation Period is two-fold. The first reason is to fulfill Daniel's prophecy of the Seventy Weeks. The second purpose Scripture gives for the Tribulation Period is that it is a period of judgment against those who reject Christ and embrace the antichrist.

Since Christians who accept Christ were already judged at the Cross, there is no role set aside for the Church in the judgments pronounced because, "Neither repented they of their murders, nor of their sorceries, nor of their fornication, nor of their thefts" (Revelation 9:21).

Repentance is a necessary condition of salvation; it is that repentance that causes us to seek forgiveness at the Cross in the first place. Since believers in the Church Age became believers by repenting, there is no purpose for bringing the judgment of an unrepentant world on the Church.

The Rapture isn't a "Great Escape," contrary to popular belief. The Rapture occurs when the restraining influence of the Holy Spirit is removed with the Church to allow the onset of the seven year period of unrestrained evil that occurs during the Tribulation (II Thessalonians 2:7).

The Rapture is the Blessed Hope of the Church, but its primary purpose is not so much a rescue mission as it is a necessary function of the withdrawal of the Holy Spirit's ministry of restraining evil. Since we are indwelt by the

Holy Spirit, when the Restrainer is withdrawn, so are we, since we are His vessels.

Therefore, it is certain to conclude that the Church won't be here for the Tribulation itself, since withdrawing the indwelling of the Holy Spirit from the believing Church would leave them spiritually defenseless at a time of maximum need; something Jesus promised He would never do.

Jesus said we could trust Him that He would never forsake His Church, and His Church is defined as being composed of believers who are indwelt by the Holy Spirit.

> And I will pray the Father, and He shall give you another Comforter, that he may abide with you *forever*. Even the Spirit of truth; whom the world cannot receive, because it seeth him not, neither knoweth Him: but ye know Him; for He dwelleth with you, and shall be in you.[5]

(John 14: 16)

But there is no reason to conclude the Church will be raptured for the purpose of providing a *Great Escape*; as I said, the Rapture is necessary to withdrawal of the Restrainer, rather than a rescue mission to the Church.

"I will not leave you comfortless: I will come to you" (John 14:18).

Christians have suffered in every generation, and continue to suffer persecution and death for their faith today in places like Vietnam, China, Sudan and most of the Islamic world.

There is no promise to the Church of the last days for a *rescue* but rather, the Rapture is the fulfillment of an *existing* promise Jesus made; that the Holy Spirit would

69

Personally indwell believers and guide us in all truth *forever*.

> In My Father's house are many mansions: if it were not so, I would have told you. I go to prepare a place for you. And if I go and prepare a place for you, I will come again, and receive you unto myself; that where I am, there ye may be also.
>
> (John 14:2-3)

As believers, our finite understanding of *forever* begins with Pentecost and continues to the Rapture, at which point *forever* takes on its eternal meaning for all believers covered under the Covenant between Jesus and the Church.

"Wherefore comfort one another with these words" (I Thessalonians   4:18).

Chapter Three

False Christs

Is Allah God?

Until the attacks on September 11, 2001 put Islam under a spotlight, most Americans would probably have agreed with President Bush's oft-repeated statement that *Allah* is just another name for *God* and that Islam worships the same God as Christians and Jews. But this assertion makes less and less sense as we learn more about Islam and its practices.

One of the most amazing attributes of the Bible is the complete harmony between the Old and New Testaments. The Old Testament contains the Books of the Law of Moses, the history of the Jewish people, and prophecies of a coming Messiah. Mainly, the Old Testament prophesies offer the hope of a coming Messiah, whereas the New Testament is a record of the fulfillment of those prophecies.

There is a sense of linear progression in reading the Old and New Testaments. The Old Testament lays down the Law; the New Testament explains why the Law was given. Any honest reader must admit that it would be impossible to keep every element of the Ten Commandments, every waking moment of every day for an entire lifetime. In that self-admission, one finds the reason for the Law; to establish beyond all doubt mankind's need for a Savior.

Until Jesus Christ, nobody who ever lived had perfectly kept the Law. No man since has perfectly kept the Law. Perfect adherence to the Law is standard for salvation under the Law. The Book of the Law was given to prove we couldn't keep it.

Jesus' mission in the New Testament wasn't to destroy the Law, but to fulfill its purpose. Since we cannot meet His perfect standard through our own efforts, we must rely on God's grace rather than our merit. Jesus said; "For God so loved the world, that He gave His only begotten Son, that whosoever believeth in Him should not perish, but have everlasting life" (John 3:16).

The Apostle Paul explained; "I do not frustrate the grace of God: for if righteousness come by the law, then Christ is dead in vain" (Galatians 2:21).

The God of Abraham, Isaac and Jacob is a God of love; One Who understands our weaknesses and made provision for them for the express purpose of fellowshipping with us. Bible prophecy for the last days revolves around two concurrent themes; *God's Plan for the Church*, and *God's plan for the national redemption of Israel during the Tribulation Period.*

We'll discuss this in greater detail later, but our current purpose is to discuss how the Old and New Testaments harmonize. If the God of the Bible is also the God of Islam, one would expect to find that same sense of harmony in the Koran.

The Koran's God

The God of the Old Testament is revealed as a Person, intimately concerned with the affairs of men. God entered into a Covenant with Abraham, saved Noah and his family, wrestled with Jacob, and pleaded through His prophets for fellowship with His Chosen People. The God of the Old Testament sought fellowship with King David. Despite the warrior-king's blood-stained hands and sinful behavior, David was called a "Friend of God."

Allah, as revealed in the Koran is unknowable, transcendent, and disinterested in fellowship with his people. It is blasphemy to attribute personhood to Allah. The God of the Bible is a God of grace and love. Allah of the Koran is a god of war and death. The only certain way to achieve the salvation of Allah is to die in jihad.

The primary goal of God as expressed in the Old and New Testament is to spread the Gospel of peace and bring all men into fellowship with Him.

The primary goal of Allah as expressed in the Koran is to spread Islam at the point of the sword; killing all infidels who refuse to submit.

Let's make a side-by-side comparison between God as He is revealed in the Old and New Testaments and Allah, the god of Islam.

God:	Allah:
is knowable and personal	cannot be known, is far off
is revealed in three persons	is not the Father, Son nor Holy Spirit
is love	has no regard for man
is active in man's life and history	does not interact with man
is a spirit, has personality, loves, thinks, is omnipotent... etc.	is not definable, we are only told what Allah is *not*
is a God of grace	grace is not found in Allah, only judgment

Islam's Split Personality

Since the terrorist attacks of September 11, there has been a concerted effort to present a *new and improved* Islam to the world. Moderate Muslim activists in the West avoid referring to teachings that may offend Western citizens; such as the Islamic code of punishment.

They stress that they believe in Moses and Jesus. They refrain from calling Jews and Christians "infidels," "Zionists" or "Crusaders."

They use the term "Sunday School" in place of "Friday Class," and they end their speeches with the Christian expression "may God bless you."

Islam has two streams of theological thought; that based on Mohammed's sayings in Mecca and that penned from Medina. Both eventually were brought together in the Koran, but reflect two entirely different worldviews.

The Meccan view is "universalist"; it holds that Islam, Christianity and Judaism all worship the same Deity and that Moslems, Christians and Jews are all "People of the Book."

The Medina view is the narrow, conquering Islam that is reflected in the Koran by verses such as:

> O you who believe! do not take the Jews and the Christians for friends; they are friends of each other; and whoever amongst you takes them for a friend, then surely he is one of them; surely Allah does not guide the unjust people.
>
> (Sura 5.51)

Historians agree that there is a big difference between Mohammed's early religious teachings from Mecca and his later teachings, after his migration to Medina.

In Mecca Mohammed was weak, struggling to be accepted, often mocked at and ridiculed. He tried to appeal to the people of Mecca by being compassionate and loving. His teachings condemned violence, injustice and neglect of the poor.

However, after he moved to Medina and his followers grew in strength and number, he became a relentless warrior, intent on spreading his religion by the sword.

This change in Mohammed's personality becomes apparent by comparing the Meccan and the Medinan suras:

Sura 73:10 (Meccan): Allah tells Mohammed to be patient with his opponents. "Be patient with what they say, and part from them courteously."

Sura 2:191 (Medinan): Allah orders him to kill his opponents "Kill them wherever you find them, and drive them out from wherever they drove you out..."

Sura 2:256 (Meccan): Allah tells Mohammed not to impose Islam by force "There is no compulsion in religion."

In verse 193 (Medinan): Allah tells him to kill whoever rejects Islam "Fight (kill) them until there is no persecution and the religion is Allah's."

In Sura 29:46 (Meccan): Allah tells Mohammed to speak nicely to people of the Book (Christians and Jews) "Argue with people of the Book, other than evil doers, only by means of what are better! and say, we believe in what has been sent down to us and sent down to you. Our God is the same as your God, and we are surrendered to him."

Sura 9:29 (Medinan): Allah tells him to fight the people of the Book, "Fight those who do not believe in God and the last day ... and fight People of the Book, who do not accept the religion of truth (Islam) until they pay tribute by hand, being inferior."

Mohammed justified this sudden change in the Koran's mood from peaceful to militant, from conciliatory to confrontational; claiming that it was Allah who told him so.

History demonstrates what actually happened was that Mohammed grew strong in Medina - strong enough to move from being conciliatory in his approach to spreading his new religion by force, through jihad.

Those who claim to be moderate followers of Islam follow the *Meccan* Mohammed. Moslem militants follow the Mohammed of *Medina*.

Islam also teaches love, temperance and moderation. It's easy enough to prove; just read the Koran. However, since few of us ever will, the American face of moderate Islam will read it to us; as has evidently been the case with the Bush administration.

But the same Koran teaches jihad (holy war), death and destruction out of the same pages. The American face of moderate Islam will never read those passages to you. Militant Islamists, however, read them every single day; verses like:

G Men are superior to women (Sura 2:228).

G Women have half the rights of men: in court witness

(Sura 2:282) and in inheritance (Sura 4:11).

☪ A man may punish his wife by beating her (Sura 4:34).

☪ A man may marry up to four wives at the same time (Sura 4:3).

☪ A wife is a sex object for her husband (Sura 2:223).

☪ Muslims must fight until their opponents submit to Islam (Sura 9:29).

☪ A Muslim must not take a Jew or a Christian for a friend (Sura 5:51).

☪ A Muslim apostate must be killed (Sura 9:12).

☪ Stealing is punished by the amputation of the hands (Sura 5:38).

☪ Adultery is punished by public flogging (Sura 24:2).

☪ Resisting Islam is punished by death, crucifixion or the cutting off of the hands and feet (Sura 5:33).

☪ Fate decides everyone's eternal destination (Sura 17:13).

☪ Every Muslim will pass through Hell (Sura 19:71).

☪ Islamic Heaven is where a Muslim man will be reclining, eating meats and delicious fruits, drinking exquisite wines, and engaging in sex with virgins (Sura 55:54- 56) & (Sura 52:17,19).

You might notice I didn't include a lot of the "moderate" verses "proving" the Koran presents Islam as a religion of peace and love.

That isn't because they aren't there. It is because they are rendered meaningless by the verses that teach the opposite.

One must be an Islamic scholar to separate the Meccan verses from the Medinan verses; to know whether Allah wants them to be friends with Christians and Jews or to crucify them.

Things that are Different are *not* the Same

The god of Islam is Allah. Allah is not the God of the Christians and Jews. To be so would be an offense to Muslims. Why is that?

If Muslims believe Allah to be superior, then my differentiating between Allah and the God of the Jews means only that I follow an inferior Deity. So where is the offense?

Stating that Allah is not the God of the Christians and Jews offends Muslims because virtually everything Christians and Jews say about Islam offends Muslims. Being offended, however, is poor substitute for presenting a logical argument to the contrary. Since there *is* no logical argument to the contrary, being offended is the only recourse that remains.

Allah's teachings contradict the Bible. God says of Himself, "I change not." If God and Allah are the same Deity, then which teaching is correct?

The Bible teaches that Jesus is the Son of God. The Koran teaches that Jesus was a prophet. He was a wise man and a good teacher, but not the Son of God, since "Allah had no son."

> ...the Christians say: The Messiah is the son of Allah; these are the words of their mouths; they imitate the saying of those who disbelieved before; may Allah destroy them; how they are turned away!
>
> (The Immunity - Sura 9.30).

Jesus Christ taught that He was the Son of God and had all authority in both Heaven and earth; then went to the Cross rather than deny His Sonship.

Prophet? Jesus said He is the Son of God, God come in the flesh, the Second Person in the Trinity. Islam denies all three. How can Jesus be a prophet of Allah while teaching doctrine contrary to Allah?

Wise man? If Islam is correct, Jesus went to the Cross for a lie. If Jesus knew He was not the King of the Jews, He could have simply told the truth and Pilate would have set Him free. Not the wisest move for a *wise man.*

Good teacher? Jesus taught that His kingdom was not of this world, and that it would have no end. He forgave sins, and taught that He would rise from the dead after three days. He said He personally would return to rule the earth. These are *not* the teachings of the Koran.

If Allah had no Son, then Jesus wasn't Lord. But that would make Him a liar, and being a liar would disqualify Him as a prophet. That He would therefore have gone to the Cross for nothing effectively crushes Islamic arguments favoring His wisdom or the soundness of His teachings as logic for denying His Deity.

To rectify this inconsistency, Islam denies that Jesus died on the Cross; claiming rather that a substitute died in His place.

The Allah of Islam is not the God of the Bible. There is no sense of harmony between the Bible and the Koran, and according to the Bible, "A house divided against itself cannot stand."

Islamic apologists claim that real Islam does not endorse suicide attacks, but one can cite chapter and verse justifications for killing those who do not convert to Islam directly from the Koran.

Islam is a demanding religion, requiring great material sacrifice on the part of its adherents. So demanding is it that it is hard to imagine someone submitting to its rigid requirements if they didn't believe its teachings.

A popular counter-argument to the Koran's violence is that the Bible also contains exhortations to war, especially in the Old Testament. The Bible does give accounts of the wars of the Jews. But that is not the same as making war an element of doctrine.

> The punishment of those who wage war against Allah and His apostle and strive to make mischief in the land is only this, that they should be murdered or crucified or their hands and their feet should be cut off on opposite sides or they should be imprisoned; this shall be as a disgrace for them in this world, and in the hereafter they shall have a grievous chastisement...
>
> (The Dinner Table, Sura 5.19)

The facts are these. The philosophy (or spirit) of Islam is at war with the philosophy (or Spirit) of Judeo-Christianity. Not all Americans are Christians or Jews, but all Americans are declared enemies of the al-Qaeda terrorist network. *All* of al-Qaeda is Muslim.

Does this reasoning lead to the syllogism, "all Muslims are al-Qaeda"? Of course not. Does it prove that all Muslims are enemies of America? Not quite. But Muslims who are not enemies of Christians and Jews are not quite fully Muslim either - if one is to believe the Koran.

This reasoning does, however, establish a logical truth even more dangerous; there is no way to tell who is what.

Not until after it is too late.

The "Sudden" Rise of Radical Islam

Have you ever watched the news and wondered just where the heck all these Islamic terrorists come from, anyway?

Twenty years ago, most of us were only peripherally aware of Islam and pretty much all we knew about them politically was that they hated Jews.

Regarding Islam as a religion, most of us were content to include it as one of the world's Three Great Monotheistic Religions, and we assumed that Muslims worship the same God as Christians and Jews.

That is, if we even gave Islam a thought, back in 1986. It was so far under the radar that, to most Americans, Islam just appeared out of nowhere.

As far as *radical* Islam is concerned, as far as most of us were concerned, that was the only kind there was. The only Islam we ever heard about was radical Islam.

It was Islamic radicals that took over the US Embassy in Tehran in 1977. It was Islamic radicals that blew up the US Marine Barracks in Beirut in 1983. Islamic radicals hijacked an airplane every couple of years or so, but that was about the only introduction to Islam most of us ever had.

None of us knew much about Islam until after September 11 - but it hasn't left the front page news since. Isn't it worth asking ourselves, how could something so powerful and so dangerous have escaped our notice for so long?

And why its sudden rise at *this* particular point in history?

Giant Flying Fire-Breathing Donkeys

Christians who study Bible prophecy and interpret it literally are generally dismissed as "prophecy nuts" by *mainstream* Christianity and marginalized as "doom merchants" or something less flattering.

Most Christians would be surprised to know that eschatology (the study of *last things*) is one of the three major principles of Islam.

Eschatology is even more central to Islam than it is to Christianity. And they take it much more seriously.

Islamic eschatology includes a second coming of Jesus, except that Islam's Jesus isn't Christ, but a prophet. At a time appointed by Allah, *Isa* (Islam's Jesus) will return to earth physically and join forces with the *Mahdi* (more on this character later) during the Islamic version of the Tribulation.

Together, they will defeat the infidel hordes. *Isa* finally kills *ad-Dajjal* (Islam's antichrist) and ushers in the Messianic era. *Dajjal* means "false prophet" or "imposter."

Islamic eschatology follows the basic New Testament outline for the last days in many respects, although the description of the *Dajjal* sounds like a comic book character.

> He will be physically misshapen, and will be blind in his left eye. His right eye will be present but it will be dark (black). In a number of hadith he is referred to as one-eyed. He will ride a giant white donkey whose each step will span a mile, will eat fire and exhale smoke, fly over land and cross seas.[1]

Giant, flying, fire-eating donkeys aside, Islamic eschatology plays a big role in radical Islamic thinking.

Reading the Signs

The Islamic world is looking at the same signs of the times that we are and reaching the same conclusions. The only places where we differ are in the details.

That is one of the reasons for what appears to us to be the *sudden* appearance of Islam on the world's stage.

It explains why radical Islam seems to be everywhere; Afghanistan, Saudi Arabia, Pakistan, Syria, Iran, Iraq, Turkey, the Russian "Stans," Egypt, Indonesia, India, across Europe. It would be shorter to list the countries where radical Islam does *not* have a foothold.

Islamic eschatology follows the basic Bible outline for the last days. It's not surprising then, that Muslims, seeing end-times events unfold before them validate all Islamic prophecy as divinely inspired.

Since they believe these are the last days, they expect the *Mahdi* to soon appear on the scene to lead them in glorious victory.

The *Mahdi* can't lead an army of jihadists to glorious victory without first having an army to lead. That world-wide jihadist army is already in place and growing exponentially as the Muslim world prepares for its own version of the Tribulation.

The Armageddon Clock

In the first half of the 20th century, the world's Jews began responding to an irresistible call to return to the Land of Promise; as the Bible said they would in the last days. With the restoration of Israel, the countdown clock to Armageddon began ticking.

The Last Generation

In the last half of the 20th century, the Islamic world began responding to an equally irresistible call to mobilize for jihad in accordance with Islamic-inspired belief that these are the last days.

The Jews believe these are the last days. The Muslims believe these are the last days. Each reached their conclusions independently based on the study of their own scriptures and comparing them to the signs of the times.

Islam's Mahdi

Among most anticipated events in Islamic eschatology is the coming of a man known as, "The Mahdi." The coming of the Mahdi is the crowning element of all Islamic end-time narratives.

Iranian president Mahmoud Ahmadinejad believes that an Islamic war against the West will hasten the Mahdi's return and has said so publicly, on more than one occasion.

According to Muslim tradition, the Mahdi will ride forth on a white horse at the head of his forces.

In their book, _Al Mahdi and the End of Time_, Muhammad Ibn 'Izzat and Muhammad 'Arif, popular Egyptian authors, identify the Mahdi from the Book of the Revelation:

> "I find the Mahdi recorded in the books of the Prophets...For instance, the Book of Revelation says: 'And I saw and behold a white horse. He that sat on him...went forth conquering and to conquer.'"

'Izzat and 'Arif then go on to say:

> "It is clear that this man is the Mahdi who will ride the white horse and judge by the Qur'an (with justice) and with whom will be men with marks of prostration on their foreheads."

Compare this to Bible prophecy:

> And he causeth all, both small and great, rich and poor, free and bond, to receive a mark in their right hand, or in their foreheads.
>
> (Revelation 13:16)

Unmasking the White Horseman

Islam holds that the Mahdi is the rider on the white horse, the first of the "Four Horsemen of the Apocalypse."

While there may be a *moderate* Islamic majority lurking out there somewhere, the Mahdi is as central to Islamic eschatology as the Second Coming of Christ is to Christianity.

The Mahdi, according to Islam's own scholars, is identified in the Christian Bible!

> ...behold a white horse: and he that sat on him had a bow; and a crown was given unto him: and he went forth conquering, and to conquer...And there went out another horse that was red: and power was given to him that sat thereon to take peace from the earth, and that they should kill one another: and there was given unto him a great sword.
>
> (Revelation 6:2, 4)

Who, then, is the rider of the white horse in Revelation 6? The consensus of mainstream Bible commentaries says the rider on the white horse is the antichrist.

The Culture of Death

One of the major failings of the Bush administration has been to minimize Islam's role in the war against terror; adopting the mantra that "Islam is a religion of peace hijacked by a few murderers" instead of investigating the religion's core teachings.

Before a gathering of ambassadors in the East Room of the White House on the first anniversary of the Iraq War, President Bush noted; "On a tape claiming responsibility for the atrocities in Madrid, a man is heard to say, 'We choose death, while you choose life.'"

But not once in his speech did Bush mention the reason for the terror. The reason is Islam itself. It is Islam that requires all faithful Muslims to conquer the world for Islam, either by voluntary conversion or submission under the sword.

Islam is at war, first of all with itself, and secondarily with the rest of the world.

Within Islam are two major sects, the Sunnis and the Shia. Sunnis claim Islam descended directly from Mohammed, while the Shia say the true succession of Islam came through Ali, married to the prophet's daughter, Fatima.

The eight year war between Iran and Iraq during the 1980's was essentially a war between Sunni Islam and the Shia Republic of Iran. When US forces invaded Iraq, they discovered hundreds of mass graves containing the bodies of tens of thousands of Shiite Iraqis murdered by Saddam's Sunni-dominated military.

Judaism and, by extension, Christianity claim their spiritual heritage is descended from Abraham, through the line of Isaac and Jacob.

Islam claims its heritage through Abraham's elder son, Ishmael. Of Ishmael, Genesis 16:12 tells us; "And he will be a wild man; his hand will be against every man, and every man's hand against him; and he shall dwell in the presence of all his brethren."

Islam is a religion born out of blood and the sword, not peace. The secular Muslim scholar Ibn Warraq, author of *Why I Am Not a Muslim* and *The Quest for the Historical Muhammad*, points out that, from the approved holy books on the life of Mohammed that the prophet and his band of followers participated in 80 political assassinations in their consolidation of power.

"Remember Andalusia"

During the 8th century, Islam conquered a wide swath of territory from the Arabian Peninsula all the way to the Iberian Peninsula, which it called "Andalusia"; the area known today as Spain.

To Muslims this entire area is part of the *Dar al Islam*, the *Zone of Submission*. It is a received doctrine of the Koran that no part of the *Dar al-Islam* ever can be ceded permanently to the infidel. The Moors were kicked out of Andalusia in 1493 by the Spanish Reconquest. But Islam has a long memory.

On Oct. 7, 2001, the day the United States began bombing Afghanistan, Osama bin Laden appeared in a videotape, stating; "Let the whole world know that we shall never accept that the tragedy of al-Andalus would be repeated."

While areas conquered by Islam are known as *Dar al Islam*, areas unconquered by Islam all fall under *Dar al-Harb*, the *Zone of War*. Islam demands an armed struggle to bring the rest of the world under the *Dar al Islam*, offering conversion or the sword. This is a basic principle of Islam; the "religion of peace."

A Little Hash, A Little Nosh…

We get our word *assassin* from a twelfth century Islamic forerunner of Osama bin-Laden named *Hasan-i Sabbah*. His terrorist group, "the Ismalis," served as the model for al-Qaeda's secret society.

Called the "Old Man in the Mountain" Hasan-i Sabbah attracted hundreds of young men by offering training in religious doctrine, devotional discipline and terrorism. He singled out for attack those rulers he judged to have been corrupted by power and luxury or who, in his view, were insufficiently dedicated to the principles of Islam.

His followers would steal into palaces in the dead of night and slit the throats of their victims; knowing in the process, that they would be caught and killed. This disadvantage was offset by a carefully taught theology that, when slain, they would be rewarded instantly with the joys of paradise.

These terrorists were called assassins, or, the *Hashishiyyin*, because they used hashish to bolster their courage.

According to accounts brought back by the Crusaders, the *Old Man in the Mountain* had such control over his followers that he would amuse and terrorize visitors to his castle by ordering a few of his young men to jump off a cliff to demonstrate that they would obey his slightest whim.

Islam is first and foremost, a culture of death, not life. To its adherents, the highest possible honor is to die a "shaheed" (martyr) in battle with the infidel enemy. To die in battle in jihad is the one iron-clad guarantee of heaven in Islamic theology. When a family member achieves *shaheed*, the family holds a celebration and hands out sweets.

Attorney General John Ashcroft once famously observed that; "Islam is a religion in which God expects your son to die for him. Christianity is a religion in which God sent His Son to die for you."

CHAPTER FOUR

WARS AND RUMORS OF WARS

> And ye shall hear of wars and rumours of wars: see
> that ye be not troubled: for all these things must come
> to pass, but the end is not yet. For nation shall rise
> against nation, and kingdom against kingdom: and
> there shall be famines, and pestilences, and
> earthquakes, in divers places. All these are the
> beginning of sorrows.
>
> (Matthew 24:5-6)

The verses quoted above were part of Jesus' response to
the question, "What will be the sign of Thy coming and of
the end of the world?"

The Lord's reply to the question is known to Bible scholars
as the "Olivet Discourse" because Jesus was standing
"upon the Mount of Olives" at the time. His answer, which
is contained in all three Synoptic Gospels, fills the entire
chapter. It is one of Jesus' lengthiest teachings in the New
Testament.

The Olivet Discourse focuses its attention on events that
take place *during the tribulation,* but begins by describing
the events that conspire together to bring it about.

The period of wars and rumors of wars has been ongoing
now since 1914 with the first truly global war in human
history. It was followed by a second global war in 1939,
whose conclusion brought about the ultimate "rumor of

war," the cold war between the West and the Soviet Empire.

Two different entities are under discussion; *nations* and *kingdoms*. The word *nation* is translated from the Greek word "ethnos" and describes an ethnic state, like Israel or one of the ethnic states of the Arab world. Or North Korea.

The world translated *kingdom* - "basileia" means "royal power, kingship, dominion, rule" and it describes a national entity bound together by socio-economic interests, rather than ethnic relationships.

America would fit the Biblical understanding of a *kingdom* in the sense Americans are not bound together by blood or ethnicity, but rather by common social and economic benefits. The same could be applied to the member states of the EU. Individually, some European countries might be ethnic in origin, but the Common Market exists for economic reasons.

The collapse of the Soviet Union uncorked a new round of ethnic unrest and international conflict, but, as Jesus was careful to note, "the end is not yet."

Birth Pangs

Ethnic or economic strife has been responsible for all the wars of modern times. While the World Wars were aimed primarily at conquest for economic reasons, Hitler's Nazis sought both ethnic purity and "lebensraum" (living space) for Germany.

Japan's Imperial government set out to conquer Asia to ensure a steady supply of raw materials and to establish ethnic Japanese rule over Greater Asia.

Skeptics might argue that wars, ethnic unrest, even famines, earthquakes and pestilences, all have been part of the human condition since the Fall of Man at the Garden of Eden.

Note that Jesus said "all these are the beginning of sorrows." The word *sorrow* first appears in Scripture in Genesis 3:16 when God told Eve, "I will greatly multiply thy sorrow and thy conception; in sorrow thou shalt bring forth children." *Sorrow* is translated from the Hebrew "itstsabown" and refers to labor pains.

The Greek word "odin" translated as *sorrows* in Matthew 24:8 also refers to labor pains.

Every parent who has ever lived could instantly grasp the meaning of this metaphor - that is why Jesus chose it. As the birth of a child approaches, the mother begins to experience labor pains, which, having once begun, continue to increase in both frequency and intensity as the moment of birth approaches.

Prospective parents in Jesus' day did exactly what I did with each of my kids timed the interval between the contractions. "Labor pains" was a carefully chosen metaphor designed to resonate with all people, of all cultures, in all generations. But, to the generation to whom those signs were addressed, the meaning would be unmistakable.

The Nuclear Threat

North Korea has the capability to deliver a nuclear warhead to a target five thousand miles away. All of Europe is within reach of Pyongyang, as is Japan and the extreme west coast of Alaska.

And the North Koreans are as likely to supply al-Qaeda with a nuclear weapon as Saddam was to give them biological or chemical weapons.

A terrorist with a chemical or biological agent would have the potential to kill thousands. A terrorist with a nuclear weapon is almost unthinkable.

The following is a scenario, assuming a one-kiloton ground blast somewhere in the United States. Let's select Niagara Falls, since it is one of the world's most recognizable locations.

A strike against Niagara Falls would reverberate around the globe. It is also a *soft target*, since it borders with Canada.

Suppose a suicide *jihadist* detonated a nuclear device hidden in the trunk of his car somewhere beside the Falls?

Where the mighty Niagara once roared majestically, there would be a hole 200 feet deep and 1000 feet in diameter.

Before the blast, the water going over the Falls dropped 166 feet into the Niagara Gorge. Its entire area was less than a thousand feet across. After the blast, the Falls are entirely obliterated within the blast crater.

Nothing recognizable remains within about 3,200 feet (0.6 miles) from the blast center, except perhaps, the remnants of some building foundations.

At 1.7 miles, only some of the strongest buildings - those made of reinforced concrete - are still standing. Ninety-eight percent of the population in this area is dead.

The Niagara Falls power generating plant is gone. Much of the Eastern seaboard of the United States has gone dark.

Within a circle of 2.7 miles, virtually everything is destroyed. The walls of typical multi-story buildings, including apartment buildings, have been completely blown out. The bare, structural skeletons of more buildings rise above the debris as you approach this ring. Single-family residences within this area have been completely blown away - only their foundations remain.

Fifty percent of the population in this area is dead. Of the survivors, forty percent are injured. The cities of Niagara Falls on both sides of the border are utterly destroyed.

Within a radius of 4.7 miles, any single-family residences that have not been completely destroyed are heavily damaged. The windows of office buildings have been blown away, as have some of their walls.

The contents of their upper floors, including the people who were working there, are scattered on the street. A substantial amount of debris clutters the entire area. Five percent of the population in this ring is dead. Again, forty percent of the survivors are wounded.

At 7.4 miles in all directions from what moments ago was the mighty Niagara, residences are moderately damaged. Commercial buildings have sustained minimal damage. Twenty-five percent of the population in this ring has been injured, mainly by flying glass and debris.

Many others have been injured from thermal radiation - the heat generated by the blast. The remaining seventy-five percent are unhurt.

The scenario above, according to a 1979 government report entitled "The Effects of Nuclear War,"[1] is based on a one-kiloton nuclear detonation with Niagara Falls at Ground Zero.

The nuclear suitcases that went missing in 1991 from the former Soviet Union have a yield of 0.6 megatons and weigh about sixty pounds. It is rumored that Osama bin Laden may have bought as many as twenty of them from Russia's Chechen rebels.

North Korea currently has enough plutonium to construct four or five one-kiloton nuclear devices that would fit in a car trunk.

This scenario, as horrible as it is, is entirely plausible. But it is not the only rumor of war worrying the planet.

"Star Wars"

One of the US military programs that is most credited with the eventual collapse of the Soviet Union was Ronald Reagan's "Star Wars" missile defense system. The US never actually even put it up - the mere threat was enough.

For forty years, the doctrine of *Mutually Assured Destruction* (appropriately known by its acronym, *MAD*) guaranteed both the Soviets and the West that neither power would use its nuclear arsenal because it would mean their own national suicide.

"Star Wars" envisioned using satellites to pinpoint and shoot down incoming nuclear ICBM's. A US missile shield would theoretically nullify a Soviet nuclear retaliation, rendering the doctrine of *Mutually Assured Destruction* obsolete.

The Soviet Union collapsed because it couldn't afford to build a system that could defeat "Star Wars"; making Soviet countries vulnerable to a US nuclear first-strike.

The Soviets faced a choice; dissolution or destruction. They chose the former; and the rest, as they say, is history.

In January 2007, the People's Republic of China successfully conducted a missile test that could render "Star Wars" as obsolete as Snoopy's Sopwith Camel biplane. [2]

China Goes Ballistic

The Chinese fired a ballistic missile into space, targeting an obsolete Chinese weather satellite orbiting roughly 530 miles above the earth. First, let's make sure we all understand the definition of a "ballistic" missile.

According to the dictionary:

> A ballistic missile is a missile, usually with no wings or fins, with a prescribed course that cannot be altered after the missile has burned its fuel, whereafter its course is governed by the laws of ballistics. [3]

In other words, a bullet is a type of ballistic missile. It has no guidance after it has expended the fuel that propels it from the muzzle. Once in flight, it goes where it was aimed before it was fired.

Let that sink in for a second.

What China did, in essence, was take aim at a four foot by four foot weather satellite traveling at seventeen thousand miles per hour in its orbit 530 miles above the earth.

The KT-2 missile is little more than a giant, unguided bullet that goes where it is aimed. But China scored a bull's-eye with its first shot.

Although Reagan's "Star Wars" never got off the ground, the US is currently developing a next-generation version, called the US National Missile Defense program. It is a network of rocket interceptors and computers guided by satellites and designed to protect America from incoming missile attack.

The "Star Wars" program was scrapped after the collapse of the Soviet Union because the US no longer deemed it necessary. In the 1990's the Clinton administration admitted that Reagan's "Star Wars" project wouldn't have worked anyway against the vast Soviet arsenal of more than 27,000 nuclear weapons.

But the new program, nicknamed "Son of Star Wars" was ordered by the Bush administration as a defense against nuclear attack by rogue nations like North Korea or Iran. Or China...whose nuclear arsenal is currently believed to number only in the teens.

Getting By With a Little Help from Our Prez

As part of a 1989 sanctions package meant to punish Beijing for the massacre of students in Tiananmen Square, Senator Al Gore sponsored legislation barring US-made satellites from being launched on Chinese rockets - unless the President declared such a launch to be in the national interest.[4]

In 1996 a Chinese-made rocket carrying an American-made Loral satellite into space exploded in flight[5].

In the aftermath, Loral and another firm, Hughes Electronic Corporation, gave technology to the Chinese that, according to the Pentagon, fixed a major guidance system problem. This guidance system technology also affected China's ICBM arsenal.

The Chinese military obtained encrypted radiation hardened chips from Loral, post-boost vehicle technology from Lockheed, telemetry systems from Motorola and nose cone technology from Hughes.

Chinese generals made huge profits from the advanced rocket and satellite deals - so did Loral.

Bernard Schwartz, Loral's chairman, requested a presidential waiver, after the fact, to protect Loral from criminal prosecution for transferring the technology. Schwartz, coincidentally, was the largest individual donor to the Democratic National Committee in 1996; responsible for more than $600,000 in soft-money donations to the Clinton-Gore campaign.[6]

According to a February 18th decision memo, Clinton was warned that the Justice Department believed that, should the Loral investigation go to trial, "a jury likely would not convict" if the company received another presidential waiver. How serious could the breach be if the White House approved yet another technology transfer?[7]

By signing the waiver, Clinton handed his donor's company a *get-out-of-jail-free* card and handed China the ability to destroy America.

The Loral-supplied technology represented a major breakthrough for the Chinese military. China has been increasing its military capabilities ever since.

Since the mid-1990's China has expanded its short and medium range ballistic missile systems for use against US aircraft carriers. China has also invested heavily in nuclear submarines; having launched more than sixty new subs in the past five years. Beijing is also currently constructing its first aircraft carrier.

Chinese military spending more than doubled since the Clinton waiver was granted in 1996 and is estimated to be second only to the United States in the percentage of its GDP spent on military development.[8]

China has been strengthening ties with America's enemies, particularly Iran and North Korea. The majority of Third World ballistic missile arsenals are based on designs proliferated by China.

The January 2007 ballistic missile test shows that the Chinese could soon have the capability to destroy the array of commercial satellites operated by the US, Europe, Israel, Russia and Japan.

In testimony before Congress, Lt. General Michael Maples, head of the US Defense Intelligence Agency, warned that "Russia and China continue to be the primary states of concern regarding military space and counter-space programs."[9]

Other countries, he said:

> ...continue to develop capabilities that have the potential to threaten US space assets, and some have already deployed systems with inherent anti-satellite capabilities, such as satellite-tracking laser range-finding devices and nuclear-armed ballistic missiles.

Since they travel at an even lower orbit than the weather satellite China hit with its first shot, the test proves that Beijing can now take out US spy satellites at will.

The Chinese military also makes no it secret that it would welcome a nuclear war with the United States - a war that China believes it could win.

According to an August 1999 policy document published by the People's Liberation Army Office of China's Central Military Command[10]:

> ...unlike Iraq and Yugoslavia, China is not only a big country, but also possesses a nuclear arsenal that has

long since been incorporated into state warfare system and play a real role in our national defense.

In comparison with the U.S. nuclear arsenal, our disadvantage is mainly numeric, which in real wars the qualitative gap will be reflected only as different requirement of strategic theory," says the Chinese military document.

In terms of deterrence, there is not any difference in practical value. So far we have built up the capability for the second and third nuclear strikes and are fairly confident in fighting a nuclear war. The PCC [communist Party Central Committee] has decided to pass though formal channels this message to the top leaders in the U.S.

And the overwhelming assessment by officials in the region, including Australia, Japan and South Korea, is that the US military could not defeat China. Although most Asian officials have kept their assessments private, Tokyo Governor Shintaro Ishihara went public, warning that the United States would lose any war with China.

In an address to the Washington-based Center for Strategic and International Studies, Mr. Ishihara said:[11]

In any case, if tension between the United States and China heightens, if each side pulls the trigger, though it may not be stretched to nuclear weapons, and the wider hostilities expand, I believe America cannot win as it has a civic society that must adhere to the value of respecting lives.

Ishihara said US ground forces would be unable to stem a Chinese conventional attack. Indeed, he asserted that China would not hesitate to use nuclear weapons against Asian and American cities - even at the risk of a massive US retaliation.

The Last Generation

The governor said the US military could not counter a wave of millions of Chinese soldiers prepared to die in any onslaught against US Forces. It is worth noting that China could afford to lose as many as 200 million men and would still have more forces in reserve than the US military has in total.

> And the number of the army of the horsemen were two hundred thousand thousand: (200 million) and I heard the number of them…. By these three was the third part of men killed, by the fire, and by the smoke, and by the brimstone, which issued out of their mouths.

> (Revelation 9:16, 19)

Mahdi Rising

The Islamic Republic of Iran Broadcasting Company (IRIB) ran a television series called *"The World Toward Illumination"*[12] which outlines the signs of the times for the Islamic faithful and what to expect when the Islamic messiah arrives.

In America, we have dozens of such television programs. Messianic websites (like the author's: *www.omegaletter.com*), and books dedicated to the signs of the times proliferate.

So, why should Iranian TV broadcasting similar programming be worthy of note?

Two reasons immediately leap to mind. The first is the fact there is a sense of messianic imminence in the Islamic world. An equally intense expectation of the coming Messiah exists among the religious Jews.

Banners proclaiming the coming of the Messiah festoon Jerusalem and its environs. Gershon Salomon, head of the Temple Mount Faithful, told me at his home in Jerusalem back in 1992 that he expected to witness the coming of the Jewish Messiah. The organization he founded in 1967 is dedicated to rebuilding the Temple, a prerequisite of the Jewish Messiah's return.

Although much of mainstream Christianity is divided in their understanding of Bible prophecy, there is a growing sense within the faith that the Apocalypse is just around the corner.

Awaiting the Apocalypse

In a New Year's AP poll, respondents were asked for their predictions for 2007. Seventy percent predict a major natural catastrophe. Sixty percent anticipate a major terror attack. Thirty-five percent predict a cure for cancer, the same number predict the reinstatement of the military draft.

Among the predictions, a startling twenty-five percent, one in four Americans, predicted 2007 would see the Second Coming of Christ.

One in four! Let's try and put that into context. Consider the clout of the US anti-God lobby. Kids can't pray in public. The Ten Commandments can't be displayed in public. The Bible is banned from public display, and has been called "hate literature" by the courts. All this, yet US atheists number less than ten percent of the population.

Let's consider the clout of the US Muslim lobby. Muslim leaders enjoy an open-door policy with the White House. Any Muslim who complains of discrimination gets instant national headlines. But US Muslims account for less than three percent of the population.

Now, reconsider the fact that *twenty-five percent* of the participants of a poll representing US national opinion, share the common vision of a coming apocalypse; as do Muslims and Jews.

The second reason that Iranian TV broadcasting programs relating to the signs of the last days is a big deal, is rooted in the differences between Judeo-Christian and Islamic eschatology.

Jews expect the Messiah to usher in an era of peace and security. Christians expect the Messiah to return and set up a Kingdom of peace and security that will last a thousand years.

Islam's messiah returns to lead a conquering Islamic army to wipe the Jews and Christians from the face of the earth.

While Christians who study Bible prophecy find it a source of inspiration and hope, Islamic eschatology offers blood and death. Iran's *"World Toward Illumination"* notes the Mahdi will soon "form an army to defeat Islam's enemies in a series of apocalyptic battles" and "will overcome his arch villain in Jerusalem."

Before the Islamic messiah appears to the world, IRIB reports, "a pious person ... a venerable God-fearing individual from Iran" will meet with the Mahdi. This individual will pledge allegiance to the Mahdi as he "fights oppression and corruption and enters Iraq to lift the siege of Kufa and holy Najaf and to defeat the forces of (Islam's enemies) in Iraq."

Iranian TV casts its religious leadership in the role of the "pious person" who will begin the apocalyptic war over Iraq that will bring about the Mahdi's return.

The program *also* takes note of Western messianic expectations, but claims it is the Christians that want to "accelerate events" to bring about the end of the world by supporting Israel.

> (O)ne of the characteristics of the West in the current era is obsession with the end of time. Experts say discussions about the savior and the "end of time," have not been so prevalent before as they are now in the west.... These extremist Christians believe that certain events must be carried out by the Protestants in the world so as to prepare the grounds for the Messiah's reappearance. The followers of this school believe they have a religious duty to accelerate these events, for example planting the illegal Zionist state of Israel for the Jews of the world, in Palestine.[13]

It has often been noted that the most effective lies are those that contain some grain of truth. Christian support for Israel is undeniably connected with Bible prophecy. *"The World Toward Illumination"* takes that one grain of truth and spins it until it justifies the destruction of Israel and an all-out war against the Christian West as a matter of religious duty.

Western negotiators with Iran don't understand their religious devotion to duty. They really think that Iran's devoutly Shiite government can be bribed, threatened or cajoled into abandoning its plans for war with the West.

Iran's ruling mullocracy fervently believe that their messiah is coming soon. Iran's current leader, Mahmoud Ahmadinejad believes with equal fervency that it is his divine mission to create the conditions that will facilitate their messiah's return.

Preparing For Armageddon

What is fascinating to me is the fact that all of these nations are preparing for what they agree will be the Battle of Armageddon.

The Last Generation

The Muslims have their own eschatological scheme for the last days, lifted from the Scriptures and then *tweaked* so that the Muslim forces come out on top in the end.

Islam awaits its own messiah figure, the *Mahdi* who will lead the forces of Islam in a victorious conquest of the world for Islam, after which everybody will live happily ever after.

Islamic scholars have even pointed to the rider on the white horse of Revelation 6:2 as the Mahdi of Islamic "prophecy" (Christian scholars identify the rider on the white horse as the antichrist).

Let's add it all up and see what we get.

In Israel, devoutly religious Jews are preparing for the coming of the Messiah. For the first time in 1,600 years, the Jewish Sanhedrin has been reconstituted, since Jewish law requires the Jewish Messiah to be certified by Israel's supreme religious court.

Gershon Salomon's Temple Mount Faithful fully expects the Messiah in the near future, and each year attempts to lay the cornerstone for the Third Temple. The Temple Mount Institute has recreated all the necessary elements for Temple worship and is training Cohanim priests in preparation.

Christians are awaiting the Second Coming of Christ in this generation. Western culture is also beginning to reflect the same expectation through books, movies and television programming.

Movies with plot lines involving the end of the world are consistent box office winners; books about Bible prophecy are best-sellers; networks like National Geographic and

A&E can't make documentaries about the Bible and the last days fast enough to meet demand.

The Islamic world is so convinced of the soon appearance of its own messiah that it is willing to bring about a global conflagration in order to hasten his appearance.

So we have the world's three largest monotheistic religions all convinced at the same point in history that this is the generation of the messiah. All three are actively making preparations in advance of his appearance.

The Jews expect their messiah to bring global peace. The Muslims expect their messiah to bring global war. The Prophet Daniel identifies the antichrist as a false messiah who rises to power by means of the promise of peace and then plunges the world into a global war of annihilation against Christians and Jews.

Revelation 6:2 pictures the rider on the white horse as carrying a bow - but no arrows (symbolic of a peaceful ascent to power), followed by the rider on the black horse that plunges the world into war.

The details remain fuzzy - since they are working themselves out in real time - but the shared expectation is crystal clear. Almost against its will, even the secular world has begun entertaining the notion that the end is near.

And they are arming themselves in preparation for it.

CHAPTER FIVE

DECEIVED

Brains: Washed, Spun-Dry and Folded...

The term "mind control" refers to the successful control of the thoughts and actions of others without his or her expressed consent.

In the most general sense, the term implies that the victim has given up some basic political, social, or religious beliefs and attitudes, and has been made to accept contrasting ideas.

Mind control, when exercised as a government policy, turned post WWI Germany from the most cultured nation in Europe into a nation of cold-blooded murderers in a single generation.

Government manipulation of facts for the purpose of controlling the population is called "propaganda." North Korea is a living example of its naked power.

North Korea's *Great Leader* Kim Il Sung and his mad progeny, *Beloved Leader* Kim Jong il, have kept North Korean society closed to outside influence for almost sixty years. Since Kim Il Sung took power in 1948, his propaganda machine has brainwashed the entire country.

Despite famines, mass starvation, *reeducation* camps, and an almost complete lack of basic necessities like electricity and clean water, the average North Korean believes his country to be one of the most advanced and desirable places to live on earth.

The late Kim Il Sung is worshipped as a god, and his son, Kim Jong il is considered by his followers, a living god. Two million North Korean soldiers stand ready to march into the teeth of battle at his whim.

Such is the power of systematic, unrestrained mind control.

It Cuts Like a Knife…

There are several ways of looking at "mind control." Some might argue that parental control over their children is a form of mind control, and the argument has logical merit.

The use of *mind control* is analogous to the use of a knife. A knife, used to take a life in a bar fight, is a bad thing. The same knife, used to save a life in performing an emergency appendectomy, is a good thing. The knife itself is neither good nor evil. It is simply a knife.

Parents' *mind control* over their children is a necessary part of maintaining the social and cultural fabric of society. Children need to be taught how to be good - being bad comes naturally, it's a product of what the Bible calls the "sin nature."

Children want to please those in authority over them, and the first thing they learn is that socially acceptable behavior earns rewards, while anti-social behavior reaps consequences. Children put this lesson it into practice; seeking to learn what is socially acceptable.

Because *mind control* is a necessary part of our learning social restrictions as children, we remain susceptible to it for the rest of our lives.

The values we learn and seek to put into practice as children - good behavior equals rewards and bad behavior equals consequences - remain with us as adults.

Nobody understands this better than the educators we trust with the power of *mind control* over our children.

Education or Indoctrination?

Two teachers with the Port Washington-Saukville School Board put together a questionnaire which was distributed to hundreds of Port Washington high school students, with instructions to submit written answers and then to discuss the survey.

The questionnaire's release was carefully timed. The survey was given to about 400 of the school's 930 students on April 25, 2006, the day before the national Day of Silence, an annual event co-sponsored by the New York City-based *Gay, Lesbian & Straight Education Network*.

According to the *Day of Silence* web site, the event is a "student-led day of action" that attempts to eliminate harassment of non-heterosexual students.

The questions students were required to submit written answers for later discussion included (*I wish I were making this up*): "If you have never slept with someone of your same gender, then how do you know you wouldn't prefer it?"

How does a high school student cope with a question like that? What possible educational value does such a question advance?

Sexual orientation aside, this is nothing less than a school system's exhortation to students to engage in premarital sex for the sake of experimentation.

Now add the question of sexual orientation to the coincidence of the *Gay and Lesbian Alliance* sponsorship, and bingo!

Our proverbial knife just got used in a bar fight.

Now, we can characterize this instance of *mind control* according to its intended use, as either good or evil.

The compulsory submission of young minds, aimed at changing existing political, social, or religious beliefs and attitudes to conform to conflicting or contrasting ideas.

Other questions on the survey included: "What do you think caused your heterosexuality?" and "When did you decide you were heterosexual?"[1]

Both were clearly designed to imply that heterosexuality is a conscious decision based on some cause - while at the same time, gay rights supporters argue that sexual orientation is neither the result of a conscious decision or caused by some external event.

If it sounds confusing to you, imagine how confusing it must sound to a fifteen-year old?

When angry parents confronted the school's principal, his response was to describe the survey as an "exercise in compassion and understanding that did not work out real well."

What it *was,* was an exercise in brainwashing. How well it worked out remains to be seen. The kids are still in high school.

Power of Delusion

The Bible says that among the most powerful weapons in the antichrist's arsenal during the Tribulation is power to delude and deceive the masses who will worship him as the messiah.

Jesus warned that the antichrist's powers of deception will be such that, if it were possible, he would even be able to deceive the very elect (Matthew 24:4).

Paul says antichrist's powers of delusion will reach their peak after the removal of the *Restrainer* (and the Church) at the Rapture.

"For the mystery of iniquity doth already work: only He who now letteth will let, until He be taken out of the way" (II Thessalonians 2:7).

Paul then speaks of those who rejected Christ and salvation during the Church Age, those with the "deceivableness of unrighteousness in them that perish; because they received not the love of the truth, that they might be saved."

Since they rejected Christ and His offer of salvation by grace through faith, "for *this* cause God shall send them strong delusion, that they should believe a lie"[2] (II Thessalonians 2:10-11).

The groundwork for that strong delusion is already being laid by predators disguised as educators; brainwashing young minds until evil and good are mere social conventions to be done away with as necessary.

The Propaganda Machine

"There are really five companies that control 90 percent of what we read, see and hear. It's not healthy." So said

CNN's Ted Turner, who spent the 1990's helping centralize that media control by merging Time, Warner Bros, CNN and AOL into the world's second largest media conglomerate.

Turner made his comments in April, 2000 while slamming the world's largest media conglomerate - NewsCorp, belonging to arch-rival Rupert Murdoch.

In an interview with the BBC, Turner said both the Israelis and Palestinians were engaged in terrorism. Only a few months after the attacks, Turner called the 9/11 hijackers "very brave."

Speaking of CNN's own audience, Turner once said, "When you've got 80 channels like you do here, people watch whatever they want. And that's the sad thing about it, because the more cerebral, the more complex, the more forward-looking the story is here in the United States, to a large extent the smaller the ratings are."

Ted Turner evidently believed CNN's ratings were slipping because the network's sophisticated political positions were beyond the grasp of the average American. He once told a forum of CNN broadcasters, "The United States has got some of the dumbest people in the world. I want you to know that. We know that."

CNN's Big Secret

During its early news coverage of the Iraq war, CNN displayed such a left-leaning bias that it drew sharp rebukes from the podiums of the Defense Department and the Pentagon. CNN, which earned the nickname the "Clinton News Network" during the 1990's, became the world's number one cable news network during this period, in part because it was the only Western media organization permitted offices in Baghdad.

After Saddam's government collapsed in April, 2003, CNN's Eason Jordan published an op-ed piece in the New York Times, entitled, "The News We Kept to Ourselves." Jordan admitted that he knew all along of the atrocities being committed by the Baghdad regime between the wars and that CNN kept quiet about it so the network wouldn't lose its offices in Baghdad.

Jordan wrote of one case in which:

> ...in the mid-1990's one of our Iraqi cameramen was abducted. For weeks he was beaten and subjected to electroshock torture in the basement of a secret police headquarters because he refused to confirm the government's ludicrous suspicion that I was the Central Intelligence Agency's Iraq station chief. CNN had been in Baghdad long enough to know that telling the world about the torture of one of its employees would almost certainly have gotten him killed and put his family and co-workers at grave risk.

It sounds like a reasonable explanation on the surface. A distasteful bit of self-censorship, but necessary to protect the innocent, in this instance. But then Jordan went on to explain that CNN had to keep on censoring anything negative about Iraq to protect all the other Iraqis on CNN's payroll. Interestingly, hardly anyone took notice of the fact that CNN took on a policy of only reporting what Iraq wanted reported.

Jordan confessed:

> An aide to Uday once told me why he had no front teeth: henchmen had ripped them out with pliers and told him never to wear dentures, so he would always remember the price to be paid for upsetting his boss.

Acceptable Deception?

Jordan's article raised an interesting question that almost nobody asked. If CNN was censoring anything Iraq didn't want reported, then wasn't CNN knowingly disseminating Iraqi propaganda and suppressing information that would make Iraq look bad? In effect, wasn't CNN serving as an arm of the Iraqi Information Ministry?

If CNN wasn't there to report the truth, then what the heck was it there for?

Although Jordan's confession was recorded in America's "Newspaper of Record" it didn't make much of a splash in the mainstream media. About the only mainstream media outlet to take notice was the conservative Washington Times:

> He *(Jordan)* wrote that Saddam's eldest son Uday "told me in 1995 that he intended to assassinate his two brothers-in-law who had defected and also... King Hussein of Jordan." The CNN news executive tipped off the king, but not the brothers-in-law, who were subsequently murdered.... So deeply had Mr. Jordan morally compromised himself and CNN that Uday the psychopath felt comfortable confiding his highest-visibility murder plans to Mr. Jordan. His secrets were safe with CNN. What a scoop they missed: "Son of Saddam Hussein plans to murder King of Jordan." Indeed, the entire Arab world might have turned on Saddam years ago if that story had been reported. But, of course, if CNN had reported that story, it would not have been able to keep open its Baghdad bureau — and thus would have lost the profitable competitive advantage it maintained over rival news outlets.[3]

Maybe the Washington Times was stretching it a bit to suggest that merely revealing a plot against King Hussein of Jordan would have caused the Arab world to turn on

Saddam. The Arab world was unlikely to be more shocked by the assassination of the King of Jordan than it was by the rapacious invasion of Kuwait.

But it seems fairly obvious that had these stories been reported freely throughout the 1990's, there wouldn't have been the kind of international opposition to the war that greeted the United States when push came to shove over invading Iraq.

Had the Arab world known what CNN knew, the arguments about "US infidels on holy Saudi territory" may have fallen on deaf ears and al-Qaeda may never have enjoyed such a fertile breeding ground.

Had Saddam's torture chambers, state sanctioned rapes, dismemberments and murders been presented by CNN with the same dedication and fervor with which it highlight Israeli "repression" of the Palestinians, al-Qaeda might not have enjoyed the popular support it gained in the Arab world.

Even the Arabs were repulsed at what they learned of life in Saddam Hussein's Iraq.

Had CNN presented the plight of the Iraqis under Saddam the way they do Palestinians under Israeli "occupation," France, Germany and Russia would have been forced to admit openly they were propping up a brutal dictatorship, instead of dancing around the issue and playing diplomatic games to stall the war and keep Saddam in power.

Instead, knowing what they knew, CNN has been the administration's chief critic of the decision to remove Saddam. Instead of focusing on the plight of Iraqis under Saddam's brutal dictatorship, CNN's war headlines focused on civilian casualties allegedly caused by errant US bombs.

Words as Weapons

A study conducted by the UCLA Political Science Department on media bias concluded in December, 2005 that, of the twenty most prominent news organizations in America, *eighteen* of them are politically biased toward the Left, and two are biased toward the right.

The UCLA study took nearly three years to complete and assessed US media coverage during the past ten years. The researchers went to great lengths to ensure against bias creeping into their study.

They made sure that as many study research assistants supported Al Gore in the 2000 election as supported President George Bush. They also sought no outside funding; a rarity in scholarly research.

Noted the study's lead author, Tim Groseclose:

> No matter the results, we feared our findings would've been suspect if we'd received support from any group that could be perceived as right or left leaning, so we consciously decided to fund this project only with our own salaries and research funds that our own universities provided.[4]

Before moving on, let's call a spade a spade. It will make things clearer as we move forward.

To be *biased to the left* means that those news organizations regularly "cook the news" in order to influence your political views to reflect Democratic values.

To be *biased to the right* means that those news organizations regularly "cook the news" in order to influence your political views to reflect Republican values.

Got it? When you turn on the news, the study found that the report you hear was specifically chosen, crafted and spun to influence your opinion of the administration specifically and that of America as a whole.

Every word is carefully selected for its maximum impact value. Facts are systematically manipulated - by design - in order to implant certain values, opinions and sympathies and to shape public opinion in a certain way.

"Media bias" sounds benign enough - especially when compared with the more accurate label of propaganda. "Bias" means "prejudice" or, "The act or state of holding unreasonable preconceived judgments or convictions."

Why am I parsing words? Because words are weapons. Weapons need to be handled carefully to make sure they don't cause unintended harm. Weapons are also used to inflict maximum damage when harm *is* intended.

The science of semantics is the linguistic equivalent to the science of war. The purpose of war is to bring about the defeat of an enemy by military means in order to impose the conqueror's will on the conquered.

Dinner for One

Semantics is the study of the impact words have on the human mind. Semantics works in linguistics the way shaped charges work in explosives.

An explosive charge can be "shaped" so that the maximum force of an explosion goes in only one direction, thereby inflicting maximum damage in only one direction.

The military anti-personnel Claymore mine is a shaped charge. Printed on one side is this helpful tip; "This Side Toward Enemy."

Now, as to how semantics uses words as *shaped charges*? Science fiction author Robert Heinlein explained it best in a short story in which one of his characters asked another rhetorically:

> Would you rather have for supper tonight? A thinly-sliced segment of muscle tissue cut from the corpse of an immature, castrated bull? Or a nice, thick, juicy steak? It's all a question of semantics.

Returning to the study: the five most left-leaning news organizations in America are the Wall Street Journal, CBS Evening News, The New York Times and the Los Angeles Times.

The two most right-leaning (and there are *only* two) are "Special Report with Brit Hume" on the Fox New Channel and The Washington Times.

Note first that there are only two "right-leaning" news organizations among the top twenty in the country. Note that "Special Report with Brit Hume" is one of them. But how far to the right is Hume's program?

It can't be too far, since it is also the fourth *most centrist* on a list in which Hume is in a statistical dead heat with the three least biased news organizations.

This isn't an endorsement of Fox News. Cooking the news is cooking the news; regardless of the underlying agenda. The bigger point is this: If one of the two most right leaning is also one of the four most centrist, then what does that say about the degree of bias inherent in the sixteen that scored lower? Not to mention the worldview of those who think they are being "informed"?

The study took things a step further; using the same formula employed by the *Americans for Democratic Action* group to rate politicians based on voting record.

The *ADA* tracks the percentage of times that each lawmaker votes on the liberal side of an issue. Based on these votes, the *ADA* assigns a numerical score to each lawmaker, where 100 is the most liberal and 0 is the most conservative.

An average ADA score of 50 is assumed to reflect the political position of the average US voter. The New York Times scored 74 making it about as liberal as Joe Liebermann. National Public Radio, a government funded news organization, was ranked the eighth most liberal of the twenty in the study.

On average, government-funded news outlets earned an ADA score of 61 (remember, 50 reflects the American mainstream).

So, the study strongly suggests that Americans have been systematically brainwashed by the mainstream media for at least ten years, with the bulk of the brainwashing effort being advanced by the liberal left.

In no instance did the study find a genuine example of a "fair and balanced" news outlet that could be trusted to reliably report just the facts without the spin.

In a nutshell, we've all been lied to for years! By the very same "free press" the Founders entrusted with the obligation to serve the public good by reporting the truth. And it doesn't seem to bother anyone.

Here's the amazing thing. I *Googled* the keywords "UCLA media bias" in its news crawler. Google returned just ten hits. I ran the same search in Yahoo News and only got six returns out of the first ten. The UCLA story didn't even come in at number one.

Britt Hume, whom the study listed among both the most right-leaning and the most centrist, mentioned the UCLA media study in his broadcast. It is the only place I've heard it reported.

He Who Owns the News, Makes the News

By digging around in the various interlocking directorates, one would discover that nineteen of the twenty news organizations included in the UCLA study belong to a handful of major multinational corporations.

Viacom, for example, as of 2004, owns CBS, UPN, MTV, Nickelodeon, Showtime, Sundance Channel, VH-1, King World Productions, Infinity Broadcasting and Comedy Central.

Viacom's holdings also include Blockbuster Video, the world's largest video rental chain, and Blockbuster Music; book publishing, including Simon & Schuster, Scribners and Macmillan; film, video and television production, including Paramount Pictures.

It holds a fifty percent interest in United Cinemas International, one of the world's largest movie theater companies. That is a lot of influence to wield over the American mind.

The owner of that influence also determines who benefits most from it. Viacom is a French-owned company.

NBC, whose twenty-nine stations reach about thirty-four percent of the national audience, belongs to General Electric. ABC belongs to the Disney Corporation. Fox News belongs to NewsCorp, an Australian news conglomerate. The fourth largest stockholder in NewsCorp is Saudi Prince Alwaleed bin Tatal.

The Saudi government is also CNN International's biggest and most lucrative advertising client. CNN's current and largest advertisers include Orascom Telecom, Qatar Airways, Lebanon Tourism, Emirates Airlines, Kuwait Fund, OPEC, Qatar Foundation and Saudi Airlines.

CNN's anti-Israel bias is so pronounced that the Israelis threatened to pull the plug on CNN in Israel as a "disseminator of anti-Israeli propaganda."

There is no such thing as an "American" media - just international corporations with international corporate interests. Interests that include Saudi oil money, expansion in international markets, and sustaining a favorable political climate for their activities and agendas back in the States.

"It's Ok. Soothe Me…"

The systematic, deliberate brainwashing of America has been ongoing for at least a decade. It is so entrenched as part of the culture now that, even when exposed for what it is, nobody really seems to care.

It is as if the public doesn't care if they are lied to or not, provided they get to choose the lie and the liars that best suit their own prejudices. It isn't being lied to that we object to - our main concern is who is doing the lying.

At the same time that all this is coming together in a single generation (none of this was even technically *possible* fifty years ago) the media propaganda machine that has been steadily concentrating itself into a single voice, has come out of the closet, so to speak. It no longer fears exposure, since they've already been exposed and nobody really cared.

So Fox News leans right and the New York Times leans left. So what? We already knew that. That's the point. Americans *know* they are being deceived - but it is okay, provided the deception fits their prejudices.

According to the Bible, in the last days, the antichrist will control everything we see, hear and do. He will order the death of the two Witnesses; "And they of the people and kindreds and tongues and nations shall see their dead bodies three days and an half" (Revelation 11:9).

The doctrine of the False Prophet reaches into every home. "...power was given him over all kindreds, and tongues, and nations..." (Revelation 13:7).

In 1950 there were 1,300 independent local newspapers. That would be a pretty unwieldy propaganda machine to control.

Today, the antichrist need only deal with the CEO's of Viacom, NewsCorp, Disney and GE.

The rest of us are lined up, like sheep for the slaughter, waiting to find out if we like what he has to say. If we like it, then it doesn't matter if it is true or not.

At least, not any more than anything else on the evening news.

CHAPTER SIX

EARTHQUAKES, FAMINES AND PESTILENCES

> For nation shall rise against nation, and kingdom against kingdom: and there shall be famines, and pestilences, and earthquakes, in divers places. All these are the beginning of sorrows.
>
> (Matthew 24:7-8)

Jesus warned that these signs were the "beginnings of sorrows." "Sorrows" is a reference to birth pangs. (Genesis 3:16, "… in sorrow thou shalt bring forth children;") Jesus used an analogy that would remain constant throughout human history. We still time labor pains. As the time approaches, the labor pains increase in both frequency and intensity.

Wars, famines and pestilences (plagues) have always been part of the human condition; until mankind declared them obsolete in the mid-20th century. We declared war on wars; setting up the United Nations as our preferred forum for settling national differences. And for a time, it worked as advertised.

We declared war on poverty; setting up programs to bring food to deprived nations and international agencies to help develop underprivileged nations.

The Last Generation

We declared war on disease; all but eradicating deadly epidemics like bubonic plague, tuberculosis, polio, malaria, leprosy and smallpox. We developed antibiotics to prevent their recurrence.

We made real progress; it looked for a while as if we might actually stamp out mankind's ancient scourges.

But that was before the appearance of antibiotic resistant "superbugs". And new diseases like HIV, AIDS and SARS. And a host of other formerly unheard of epidemics.

"Armageddon" for the Dark Continent?

According to the UN's World Health Organization, South Africa is facing a crisis it compares to *Armageddon* as a consequence of the AIDS epidemic and the nation of South Africa's national "strategy" to cope with it.

World-wide, there are roughly fifty million people infected with the AIDS virus. Twenty-seven million of them - more than half - live on the Dark Continent. South Africa has one of the highest AIDS rates in the world, with the UNAIDS agency estimating 360,000 deaths in 2001 - an average of nearly 1,000 per day.

For sub-Saharan Africa, it means that there are twenty-seven million carriers of the disease who will undoubtedly infect someone else before they die. Who will infect someone else, who will infect someone else....

There are no symptoms of AIDS infection until the disease begins to manifest itself, sometimes years after the initial infection. During all this time, the victim doesn't know he has the disease unless tested, and is unaware of the fact that he is carrying it and infecting others.

Africa is home to roughly a quarter of the world's population. Thanks to the AIDS epidemic, Africa's population is experiencing, for the first time, not zero population growth, but a negative population growth. In other words, Africans are dying faster than they are being born.[1] Unless a cure is found for the disease and made widely available, what we are witnessing is no less than the death of a continent.

AIDS is a plague unlike any in history. This is a disease that is 100% fatal, 100% of the time. Even the expensive and massive drug cocktails used by AIDS sufferers in wealthier industrialized nations don't cure the disease, but merely forestall the inevitable. But it is also a disease that has no symptoms or warning signs.

Other killer plagues of history, like the Black Death that ravaged medieval Europe, were not 100% fatal, had symptoms that uninfected people could watch for and avoid, and were confined to local geographic regions.

AIDS is the polar opposite. In addition to its mortality rate, it knows no geographic boundaries. A person infected with AIDS can hop on a plane from anywhere in the world and be in New York in a matter of hours. Where he can infect someone else who will infect someone else - you get the idea.

When asked of the signs of His coming and the end of the world, Jesus ticked off the events signaling that generation to expect His soon return. He warned first of global deception, then wars, rumors of wars, ethnic unrest, political strife, famines, pestilences and earthquakes "in divers places."

All of these things, said the Son of God, are given unto a single generation, somewhere in time, as a warning to prepare for His return. All are not only present in this generation, but are increasing in both frequency and intensity, exactly as Jesus said they would.

Pestilence means, "deadly, infectious disease" and, as unlikely as it seems, given the state of medical advancements over the past half-century, while we can cure most of the primordial killers, the risk to this generation comes from new, emerging infections like AIDS.

> And I looked, and behold a pale horse: and his name that sat on him was Death, and Hell followed with him. And power was given unto them over the fourth part of the earth, to kill with sword, and with hunger, and with death, and with the beasts of the earth.

> (Revelation 6:8)

We are not in the Tribulation now - it is a period yet to come. But the Book of the Revelation is an account of events that take place during the Tribulation, giving some sense of how close we are to that period's kickoff event.

The Rise of the Superbugs

AIDS is but one example among a host of new or mutating killer bugs. E. coli, for example, is a normal intestinal bacteria; ordinarily beneficial, suppressing harmful bacteria growth and synthesizing vitamins. A mutated strain, E. coli 0157:H7, recently emerged. Among the elderly and children, it kills half the patients it infects.[2]

Tuberculosis was the leading cause of death from infectious disease until the introduction of antibiotics in the 1950's and was all but wiped out in the 1960's. New, antibiotic resistant strains of this ancient killer have emerged that now claims the lives of almost 3,000,000 people a year world-wide.[3]

Also emerging is the penicillin-resistant Streptococcus Pneumoniae, now the leading cause of death among children, the elderly and people in poor health. Cryptosporidium parvum is another common and beneficial parasite gone mad, causing Cryptosporidiosis, for which there is no treatment and can cause dehydration and death.[4]

The Hepatitis C virus was discovered in 1988. Today almost two percent of the population is infected by Hepatitis C, which kills as many as ten thousand Americans every year.[5] And on it goes. This is nothing close to a full list of emerging killers.

There is the flesh-eating disease, *necrotizing fasciitis*, that killed puppeteer Jim Henson, not to mention new STD's (Sexually Transmitted Diseases) so terrible I won't name them, and new threats emerging all the time.

I am not much for Stephen King novels, although I admit his talent is enormous. I've read several that I liked, but I've read more that I didn't.

King is a compelling writer; its just that his chosen genre is not my cup of tea.

That said, one of Steven King's novels, _The Stand_ was made into a miniseries a few years ago. It was an apocalyptic morality tale that openly pitted good against evil.

The story begins with the emergence of a strange killer virus simply called *The Flu.*

The Flu races through the population, killing all but a handful of survivors with a natural immunity to the strain. King's depiction of the horror associated with such a pandemic certainly earned him his title as King of the

Horror Novelists - one is drawn into the story inexorably, relentlessly....

I felt much the same sense of horror as I was researching the new H5N1 "bird flu" virus that I felt reading *The Stand*.

To summarize, the bird flu known as H5N1 is shaping up to become a global pandemic on a level not seen since the 1918 Spanish Flu pandemic that swept the planet in the wake of World War One.

The Spanish Flu killed more people in six months than were killed in the four years of the First World War. It killed more humans than any other disease of similar duration in the history of the world, says Alfred W. Crosby, in his history of the 1918 pandemic.[6]

It killed so quickly that a man could be perfectly healthy one morning and be dead by nightfall. It is estimated that the death toll from the 1918 Spanish Flu was between fifty and one hundred *million* people.

H5N1 has killed more than half of those who have contracted it so far.[7] The fear is that the bird flu virus could evolve into a form that is easily spread among humans.

That could happen if a person who had a case of the ordinary human flu became infected with bird flu. The two viruses could recombine inside the victim's body, creating a hybrid transmissible between humans the way ordinary flu virus is transmitted, but with H5N1's destructive capabilities.

H5N1 is a new flu virus strain, which means that humans have no natural immunity to it. An immunity is developed when a person contracts the disease and then fights it off. If the disease never existed before, there is no way to be immune.

Because of that, its effects are more severe. There is no medicine to cure it. Antibiotics won't work. There is an experimental vaccine for H5N1. But at present, there is nowhere nearly enough to inoculate everyone against the virus - the US has a contract with Sanofi Pasteur to supply two million doses.

Since the current annual vaccine-production capacity worldwide is about 1 billion doses of the 15 microgram–antigen vaccine, right now we have the ability to produce less than enough vaccine for 100 million people in the first year of a pandemic[8] - or less than two percent of the 6.5-billion world population.

According to some experts, if avian flu becomes a pandemic, there will be two types of people in the world: those who are exposed to it and die, and those who are exposed to it and live. And put an even greater number of people at risk of succumbing to the virus.

The World Health Organization announced that H5N1 is showing signs that it can evade what is currently our first line defensive drug, *Tamiflu*. And that it has found a way to transmit itself from one human to another.

At present, the World Health Organization says "...the main route of human infection from birds is direct contact with infected poultry, or surfaces and objects contaminated by their droppings."[9]

The report came as even more bad news for doctors who already have precious little in the arsenal against bird flu should it become a human disease.

Red Flags Everywhere

Scientists say that the deadly microscopic creatures evolve to deal with antibiotics, such as penicillin, partly because doctors prescribe the medications inappropriately. When antibiotics are used for non-bacterial illnesses, or when prescriptions are not taken for the full cycle, the bugs that endure pass on their drug-resistant traits to subsequent generations.

One of the most vexing superbugs is *methicillin-resistant Staphylococcus aureus*, or *MRSA*. This bacteria used to be acquired mostly in hospitals, but now people are contracting it elsewhere. It can cause skin infections, severe bloodstream infections and even death.

Researchers at the *Baylor College of Medicine* and *Texas Children's Hospital* found that over three years, the number of MRSA infections acquired outside hospitals in Texas had more than doubled. Researchers said the study should "...raise red flags for health care workers everywhere."[10]

"There have been deaths related to this organism, although the vast number are skin and soft tissue infections," said lead researcher Sheldon Kaplan.

Researchers at the *Beth Israel Deaconess Medical Center* and *Harvard Medical School* studied the prevalence of bacteria resistant to three or more drugs over a six-year period.[11]

From 1998 to 2003, there was a significant increase in the incidence of patients carrying multi-drug resistant (MDR) bacteria when they were admitted. Three of the four species of MDR bacteria that the researchers examined, including E. coli, saw rising numbers of cases.

Rocking the House

The December 26, 2004 earthquake that spawned the Great Asian Tsunami was one of the worst natural disasters in recorded history. The earthquake that set it off was so powerful that it actually repositioned the island of Sumatra by some 100 feet to the southwest.

The quake, and the massive shift in both the earth's mass and the water covering it, actually interfered with the rotation of the earth on its axis, shortening the day by three microseconds.[12]

The tsunami killed hundreds of thousands in Asia and was so powerful that it killed hundreds of people in the African country of Somalia more than six thousand miles away from the epicenter.

The perception that earthquakes are on the increase is so widespread that the US Geological Survey felt it necessary to issue a special report entitled, *"Are Earthquakes Really on the Increase?"*

> We continue to be asked by many people throughout the world if earthquakes are on the increase. Although it may seem that we are having more earthquakes, earthquakes of magnitude 7.0 or greater have remained fairly constant.
>
> A partial explanation may lie in the fact that in the last twenty years, we have definitely had an increase in the number of earthquakes we have been able to locate each year. This is because of the tremendous increase in the number of seismograph stations in the world and the many improvements in global communications. In 1931, there were about 350 stations operating in the world; today, there are more that 8,000 stations and the data now comes in rapidly from these stations by electronic mail, internet and satellite. This increase in the number of stations and the more timely receipt of

133

data has allowed us and other seismological centers to locate earthquakes more rapidly and to locate many small earthquakes which were undetected in earlier years. The NEIC now locates about <u>20,000 earthquakes each year or approximately 50 per day.</u> Also, because of the improvements in communications and the increased interest in the environment and natural disasters, the public now learns about more earthquakes.

According to long-term records (since about 1900), we expect about 17 major earthquakes (7.0 - 7.9) and one great earthquake (8.0 or above) in any given year. [13]

Bible prophecy skeptics love to quote the USGS as evidence that Jesus got it wrong and that those who cite the rise in earthquake activity as evidence are just "merchants of doom."

In point of fact, the fact the USGS thought it necessary to publish a disclaimer is evidence that Jesus was exactly right.

And ye shall *hear* of wars and rumours of wars: see that ye be not troubled: for all these things must come to pass, but the end is not yet.... For nation shall rise against nation, and kingdom against kingdom: and there shall be famines, and pestilences, and earthquakes, in divers places. [14]

Jesus never said there would be an increase in earthquake activity. He spoke of a global *perception* that earthquakes were on the rise.

"And All the Fishes in the Sea"

The world is divided between the oceans and the land masses; five-sixths of the world's surface area is ocean. Just one-sixth of the earth's surface is dry land, and a good portion of that - mountains, deserts, polar regions, etc. are barely inhabited.

The other five-sixths of the earth's surface is covered by oceans that are miles deep in some places. The average depth of the Pacific is almost two and a half miles and the Marianas Trench is more than six miles deep. If Mount Everest were placed inside of this trench, it would disappear.

According to a 2003 report in the journal, *"Nature"* the inhabitants of one-sixth of the earth's surface have all but destroyed the inhabitants of the other five-sixths.

Only ten percent of all large fish - both open ocean species including tuna, swordfish, marlin and the large groundfish such as cod, halibut, skates and flounder - are left in the sea.

> From giant blue marlin to mighty bluefin tuna, and from tropical groupers to Antarctic cod, industrial fishing has scoured the global ocean. There is no blue frontier left.[15]

Says lead author Ransom Myers, a fisheries biologist based at Dalhousie University in Canada.

> Since 1950, with the onset of industrialized fisheries, we have rapidly reduced the resource base to less than 10 percent—not just in some areas, not just for some stocks, but for entire communities of these large fish species from the tropics to the poles.

The conclusion reached by the researchers is that the world's oceans will be completely fished out by 2048.

> At this point 29 percent of fish and seafood species have collapsed - that is, their catch has declined by 90 percent. It is a very clear trend, and it is accelerating. If the long-term trend continues, all fish and seafood

species are projected to collapse within my lifetime - by 2048.[16]

Several things in this report immediately jumped out at me. The first is that fish is the major dietary staple of some of the world's poorest countries. For more than a billion people worldwide, fish is their main source of protein.

"Behold, A Black Horse"

The Book of the Revelation tells of the Four Horseman of the Apocalypse. Of the third Horseman, Scripture says:

> ...And I beheld, and lo a black horse; and he that sat on him had a pair of balances in his hand. And I heard a voice in the midst of the four beasts say, A measure of wheat for a penny, and three measures of barley for a penny; and see thou hurt not the oil and the wine.

> (Revelation 6:5-6)

A "measure of wheat" and "three measures of barley" represent a day's food for one person. A "penny" in Scripture represents a day's wages. For the poor, the Scriptures project a time when people will work a full day to earn a day's food.

The "oil and the wine" are representative of great wealth. While the poor will face starvation, the rich will not. Globally speaking, we are almost to that point now. The gap between rich nations and poor nations has never been more pronounced.

There are places in the world today where the average annual income wouldn't buy dinner for two in a swank California restaurant. Some 2.4 billion people in the world today exist on less than $875.00 per *year*!

The second thing in the report that hit me in is the fact that, in one generation, we've depleted 90% of the ocean's fish stocks. In *one* generation. One generation from now, say scientists, there won't be any left.

The Book of the Revelation's Second Trumpet Judgment and the Second Vial Judgment both involve the death of all the fishes of the sea.

> And the second angel sounded, and as it were a great mountain burning with fire was cast into the sea: and the third part of the sea became blood; And the third part of the creatures which were in the sea, and had life, died; and the third part of the ships were destroyed.

> (Revelation 8:8-9)

> And the second angel poured out his vial upon the sea; and it became as the blood of a dead man: and every living soul died in the sea.

> (Revelation 16:3)

What an interesting *coincidence*! The Bible and secular science are predicting essentially the same result; differing only over the precise cause.

Secular science says the depletion of fish stocks began about 1950.

The Bible says the events that would lead to the fulfillment of Bible prophecy would coincide with the restoration of Israel (1948) and that all Bible prophecy would be fulfilled within that generation's lifetime.

The only real area of disagreement is the cause of the global fish-kill - both project the identical ultimate effect. And both see it coming to fruition at just about the same point in history.

The Last Generation

Mankind has relied on fish for sustenance since Adam left the Garden. Fish is synonymous with food in the Bible, and ranks up there with bread as a dietary staple.

The Bible projects two events to befall the last generation; global famine and the death of all the fishes in the sea. Secular science projects two events to befall this generation; global famine and the death of all fishes in the sea.

In 1950, the idea of running out of fish was as absurd as the idea that the Bible's last days prophecies were beginning to unfold. One generation later, both are part of the daily news.

Guardian Polar Bears and Fat Mice

The fear of an impending, global famine is so pervasive that a group known as the *Global Crop Diversity Trust* has created what was quickly dubbed "The Doomsday Vault," a cavernous concrete room carved from the side of a mountain on a frozen island located less than six hundred miles from the North Pole.

The room is designed to hold around two million seeds; representing all known varieties of the world's crops. It is being built to safeguard the world's food supply against nuclear war, climate change, terrorism, rising sea levels, earthquakes and the ensuing collapse of the electrical grid.

"If the worst came to the worst, this would allow the world to reconstruct agriculture on this planet," says Cary Fowler, director of the Global Crop Diversity Trust.

According to a report in the journal *"New Scientist"*, the Norwegian government is planning to create the seed bank next year at the behest of crop scientists.

The $3 million vault will be built deep inside a sandstone mountain lined with permafrost on the Norwegian Arctic island of Spitsbergen. The vault will have metre-thick walls of reinforced concrete and will be protected behind two airlocks and high-security blast-proof doors. It will not be permanently manned, but "the mountains are patrolled by polar bears.[17]

The new Fort Knox for the world's crops will start by taking seeds from the network of seed banks run in the Philippines, Mexico, Syria, Nigeria and elsewhere by the Consultative Group on International Agricultural Research, which is part-funded by the World Bank.

"We will then add samples from elsewhere until we have a complete set of the world's crop varieties," says Fowler.

The scheme won UN approval at a meeting of the *Food and Agriculture Organization* in Rome last October. A feasibility study said the facility "would essentially be built to last forever."

Wrote one blogger of the project:

> Let's see if they accidentally lock in there one cold-resistant pregnant mouse when they seal the place up. Then, when they open the vault years later, they can find a bunch of empty seed envelopes and about five million well-fed mice.[18]

CHAPTER SEVEN

SUN, MOON, STARS

Space Rocks, Air Bags and Armageddon

> And there shall be signs in the sun, and in the moon,
> and in the stars; and upon the earth distress of nations,
> with perplexity; the sea and the waves roaring; Men's
> hearts failing them for fear, and for looking after those
> things which are coming on the earth: for the powers
> of heaven shall be shaken....
>
> (Luke 21:28)

News headlines continue to remind us that it is only a
matter of time before the next big asteroid strike wipes us
all out; the alleged fate of the dinosaurs 85 million years
ago.

In a 2002 story with the catchy, 21st century title, *"Ready
to tackle Armageddon"* the BBC internet news reported
that the European Space Agency is planning to develop an
earth defense system to protect us all from incoming
asteroids.

A Spanish company, *Deimos-Space*, is designing the
mission and hopes its plans will convince the ESA to give
the go-ahead for a full scale test on a real asteroid. The
company has come up with a plan; the "Don Quixote"
mission, to launch a pair of probe spacecraft, Hidalgo and
Sancho, toward a far off asteroid.

One probe would hit the asteroid at extremely high speed, deflecting it slightly from its orbit.

The other would observe and make highly accurate measurements of what happened to the asteroid after the impact. The idea is that the mission would tell scientists how hard they would have to hit a real rogue asteroid heading for Earth in order to safely deflect its course.

In essence, Deimos is developing a cosmic game of 8-ball and it would like to figure out how much English to use before it's time to shoot the gameball.

If all goes according to plan, the asteroid's orbit will be shifted at impact by a few fractions of a millimeter. Tiny changes in orbit can become much larger over time and Deimos wants to use the experiment to calculate how to knock a real rogue asteroid off course.

The mission planners say that their strategy would only work if they had enough warning time, since it would take months for the Deimos Project to reach the target after launch.[1]

The plan sounds unreassuringly like the Bruce Willis movie, *"Armageddon"* (In the movie, the earth was saved - but not Bruce Willis).

That's probably why mathematician Dr. Hermann Burchard suggested a giant airbag, according to an article in *"New Scientist"* magazine. Burchard's plan is quite detailed and is generating some excitement among other mathematicians (who say the last giant asteroid hit earth 85 million years ago, but evidently failed to calculate what once in 85 million years does to the odds).

Dr. Burchard wants to inflate a giant airbag in outer space, and then steer it into the path of the oncoming asteroid with a spacecraft.

According to the Oklahoma State University professor:

> Then all you need is to take enough fuel along. You push it very gently. You don't want to push too hard because comets are very loose conglomerations of pristine matter.[2]

"It's a serious matter," said Dr. Burchard. "There is a very, very realistic threat to humanity" that would require "nations should constitute some of or other national agency to set up a defense mechanism."

2050 Party Over - Out of Time

The World Wildlife Federation has put together a report making the case that the human race is a cancer about to kill planet earth - unless some of that cancer can be excised and exported to some new host.

A report in the London Sunday Observer opens with the *unbiased* lead that the human race "will be forced to colonize two planets within fifty years if natural resources continue to be exploited at the current rate."[3] Wow!

The Observer's lead sentence is a bit startling, if you stop at the first period and read it through a couple of times. Wow!

By the time my grandson is my age, we're gonna have to find two inhabitable planets, figure out a way to get there (in less time than it would take to escape our star system, let alone discover to a new one) and send two-thirds of mankind there.

Or we are doomed. Yup. Doomed. By paragraph three, the Observer tells us that "the extra planets (equivalent to the size of Earth) will be required by the year 2050 as existing resources are exhausted."

And guess what? It's entirely our fault, say the authors, who characterized the report as a "damning condemnation of Western society's high consumption levels" (no editorial bias, there).

And just to make sure we all know that they aren't making it up, they tell us in paragraph four that the report of which they speak is "based on scientific data from across the world."

Gee! It's a good thing they got scientific data first before they told us we're doomed unless we can build *Battlestar Galactica* by 2050 or face the prospect of being forced to eat each other.

Scared Yet?

So, what's it gonna be? An armada of oil riggers preparing for a mission to destroy an asteroid on two week's notice? Or a European cosmic pool table? Or a giant air bag?

We must do something soon. After 85 billion years, there's gotta be a cosmic bullet out there somewhere with Planet Earth's name on it.

All this attention to something as provably improbable as an incoming asteroid has the conspiracy theorists abuzz: "... the governments of the world have discovered a Doomsday Asteroid coming right at us and the 'experiments' are really the real thing."

Unlikely. The only way to keep the impending destruction of the earth a secret would be if all the project scientists were shot right after they were told; before they could talk to anybody else. A strategy that wouldn't be very helpful for the long range goals of the project.

So what's all the hubbub? If the last time this happened was millions of years ago and the only survivor was a lizard that had to make the long trek through the butterfly/elephant/aardvark/platypus/ape/gorilla/scientist evolutionary process - all the way up to the beginning of recorded human history and ultimately inventing a telescope so we could scare the pants off ourselves - why the big scare now?

The real answer? Because that is what the Bible says will be the case in the last days.

In outlining events as they would unfold before that future generation, Jesus warned "... there shall be signs in the sun, and in the moon, and in the stars ..." - which accurately reflects the growing hysteria since we launched the Hubble Space Telescope and discovered how infinitely vast the universe is Scared us half to death! Which is precisely what Jesus said it would do.

As a consequence of being able to see more of the universe than ever before, we discovered that there were billions of space rocks, any one of which could hit us. All those rocks were there before; but *now* we know about them. Creating what Jesus said would cause "upon the earth distress of nations, with perplexity."

It is no stretch to see His Words reflected in today's headlines, screaming that "something must be done" to protect us from the "very realistic threat to humanity" posed by asteroid strikes.

Jesus had more to say about the likes of Dr. Burchard and the Deimos Project in the following verse:

> Men's hearts failing them for fear, and for looking after those things which are coming on the earth: for the powers of heaven shall be shaken.
>
> (Luke 21:26)

There's no doubt about it: the fear of oncoming asteroids is real. Nobody kicks out a couple of billion dollars just to practice their pool game in outer space. It is difficult to imagine *"New Scientist"* publishing an article 25 years ago, seriously proposing we build an airbag to protect us from incoming asteroids.

And there is no legitimate reason to believe, mathematically speaking, that another Big One is due, just because it's been an alleged 85 million years since the last one. How long was the interval between that one and the one before? C'mon.

Jesus was pointing out something more than simply a sudden fear of big rocks and digital telescopes. As humanity grows more arrogant in its knowledge, it grows less dependent on the defense it relied on since its beginning. Once, we simply shrugged our shoulders and said; "It's in God's Hands."

Since science claims that God no longer exists, He can no longer be trusted to protect us. Consequently, we are defenseless against space rocks.

New Age Masquerading as News

I said at the outset that the editorial agenda of the authors of the Observer article was made clear in the first paragraph.

A good writer wants to put his *wow* paragraph up front, and these guys did. The report is based on alleged "scientific evidence." The conclusions they led with are not even supported by the alleged "evidence" they cite in their article.

But by then, the reader is so distracted at the prospect of figuring out how he can arrange to be among the third that stays home while everybody else is headed to the *Planet Xenon* that the rest of the article becomes white noise.

What the World Wildlife Federation report really said was; "If all the people consumed natural resources at the same rate as the average US and UK citizen we would require at least two extra planets like Earth."

Not exactly the same as the *"we're all doomed!"* Observer lead, but probably accurate … sort of.

It depends on whether you are attempting to report news or use carefully selected *facts* to cover a propaganda piece masquerading as news.

For example, the consumption of resources is required to turn raw materials into finished goods.

Since America leads the planet in the manufacture of produced goods used globally, then it makes sense that America leads the world in the consumption of resources.

But once America consumed the raw material necessary for the global supply of left-handed widgets, there won't be any need to consume raw material to add new left-handed widgets to the existing global stockpile.

You only consume the resources to make enough left handed widgets once. After everybody that wants one has got one, the consumption ceases. For everyone to consume resources at the rate of the United States would mean everybody would be producing goods at the same pace as the United States; a conclusion completed devoid of logic.

The Last Generation

If everybody was a producer, where would the consumers come from? But the Observer treated the conclusions reached by the World Wildlife Federation as if they had been issued by NASA with the full imprimatur of the scientific community.

Each conclusion was given as a statement of undisputed fact. For example; "... either consumption rates are dramatically and rapidly lowered or the planet will no longer be able to sustain its growing population."

After making all these predictions, the authors actually cite specifics from the report to back them all up. First, there won't be enough North Atlantic cod to feed the world. Then the planetary ecosystem will get out of line.

Then animal species will be affected and start to die off. The article goes on to blame the British and Americans for being selfish pigs and squandering global resources at the expense of the Ethiopians.

You'd expect something as important as extinction might rate mention by somebody in the mainstream American scientific community.

And since the Surgeon General told us more about the dangers of second hand smoking than it has of the impending extinction of the human race, maybe it isn't as certain as these guys want us to think it is.

Believe it or not, what the Observer is advancing is a religious doctrine of the *New Age*. A basic tenet of New Age thinking is that the planet can only support a tenth of its current population.

The New Age doctrine is essentially an extreme naturalism: *Mother Earth*, "Gaia," is god. Beyond personal transformation is the New Age goal of "planetary transformation". We all are "Planetary Citizens," living in only one village, the "Global Village."

New Age is the religion of the United Nations; the guiding faith of organizations like the WWF, together with the majority of the NGOs and environmental groups that enjoy UN support.

That the Observer would run this piece of religious propaganda as news is not surprising, given the close connection between the Celtic pagan religions and the very old *New Age*.

Among New Age leading intellectuals are Richard Sutphen, Elizabeth Kubler-Ross, Benjamin Creme, Ram Das, P.D. Ouspensky, Ramtha and David Spangler. Among its evangelists are Alice Bailey, Madame Blavatsky, Al Gore, Marilyn Ferguson, Gene Roddenberry, George Lucas and Steven Spielberg.

The evangelists of the New Age worship a pantheistic god of no particular personality, one whose power is a natural force to be harnessed or released as necessary. It forms the basis for witchcraft, and is part and parcel of most pagan religions.

It is the religion of the god of this world. Marilyn Ferguson wrote in *The Aquarian Conspiracy* that she was invited to the 1982 Department of Defense annual dinner as a keynote speaker.

Ferguson identified the *National Institute of Mental Health* and the *Department of Health, Education and Welfare* as other US government institutions heavily influenced by New Age doctrine.

According to her more-than-20-year-old list, industrial giants which require their managers to attend New Age seminars include General Motors, AT&T, Chrysler Corporation, several oil companies, Lockheed and Blue Cross-Blue Shield. The list is much longer today.

The Observer's report confirms what the Bible says will be a sign of the return of Christ.

> And there shall be signs in the sun, and in the moon, and in the stars; and upon the earth distress of nations, with perplexity; the sea and the waves roaring....
>
> (Luke 21:25)

It would be fair to say the Observer's New Age propaganda piece argues in favor of *signs in the sun, moon and stars* that are bringing *upon the earth distress of nations* and most emphatically, *with perplexity*.

"Distress of Nations"

Among the most telling signs that we are approaching Zero Hour is the fear that, after six thousand years, we have used up our host planet.

A new scientific study, prepared in Washington under the supervision Robert Watson, the British-born chief scientist at the World Bank and a former scientific adviser to the White House warns that very thing.

According to the study, human civilization has consumed two-thirds of the world's resources, most of it in just the last sixty years. Among its findings:

• Because of human demand for food, fresh water, timber, fiber and fuel, more land has been claimed for agriculture in the last 60 years than in the 18th and 19th centuries combined.

• An estimated 24% of the Earth's land surface is now

cultivated.

• Water withdrawals from lakes and rivers have doubled in the last 40 years. Humans now use between 40% and 50% of all available freshwater running off the land.

• At least a quarter of all fish stocks are over harvested. In some areas, the catch is now less than a hundredth of that before industrial fishing.

• Since 1980, about 35% of mangroves have been lost, 20% of the world's coral reefs have been destroyed and another 20% badly degraded.

• Deforestation and other changes could increase the risks of malaria and cholera, and open the way for new and so far unknown disease to emerge.

• Flow from rivers has been reduced dramatically. For parts of the year, the Yellow River in China, the Nile in Africa and the Colorado in North America dry up before they reach the ocean.

• An estimated 90% of the total weight of the ocean's large predators - tuna, swordfish and sharks - has disappeared in recent years.

• An estimated 12% of bird species, 25% of mammals and more than 30% of all amphibians are threatened with extinction within the next century. [4]

This report is stunning, (even though it is sure to be disputed by other, equally qualified environmental scientists). Let's revisit the fact that we've been on this planet for at least six thousand years. But it is *this* generation has allegedly used it up.

It is *this* generation in which men's hearts have begun to fail them "for fear, and for looking after those things which are coming on the earth."

Signs in the sun, moon and stars have astronomers baffled. Fears of a catastrophic collision with giant space rocks have us scanning the heavens and planning our defense from a threat that we didn't even know existed a generation ago.

The "distress of nations" is palpable; witness the panic that ensued after the latest undersea aftershock as millions fled a new killer wave that never arrived.

The study says that we are running out of food sources, out of fresh water, and we face the threat of killer plagues and epidemics; we've over fished the oceans and destroyed the seabed.

And the study concludes all this damage took place - not gradually over six thousand years of human existence - but within a single generation!

UN Report: The Beginning of Sorrows

According to a report issued in September, 2004, by the United Nations disaster reduction agency, (UN/ISDR), there has been a global spike in world-wide natural catastrophes, as well as those of the man-made variety.

More than 254 million people were affected by natural hazards in 2003, a near three-fold jump from 1990, according to data released by the inter-agency secretariat.

And a long-term trend over the past decade shows a steady rise in victims, according to the statistics from the Centre for Research on the Epidemiology of Disasters at the University of Louvain in Belgium.

"Not only is the world globally facing more potential disasters, but increasing numbers of people are becoming vulnerable to hazards," says the UN/ISDR report. [5]

The report notes that disasters ranging from storms, earthquakes and volcanoes to wildfires, droughts and landslides killed some 83,000 people in 2003 compared with about 53,000 deaths thirteen years earlier.

In addition, storms and freak temperatures appear to be on the rise with 337 natural disasters reported in 2003, up from 261 in 1990.

An onslaught of deadly hurricanes that have battered the southern United States support theories that such storms are occurring more frequently.

"Look at the number of hurricanes this year, it is hard to keep up with all the names," said the UN/ISDR's John Harding.

> The scientific community tells us that the intensity and frequency of disasters are very likely to increase in the medium-term due to climate change and that increase may well be occurring at this stage.[6]

The Earth is Bi-Polar!

According to a report in the Science section of the New York Times we are perhaps 150 years into the collapse of the Earth's magnetic field.[7]

William Broad writes that the field's strength has waned ten to fifteen percent, and the deterioration has accelerated of late, increasing debate over whether it portends a reversal of the lines of magnetic force that normally envelop the Earth.

During a reversal, the main field weakens, almost vanishes, and then reappears with opposite polarity. According to Broad, the magnetic field reversal will take hundreds, if not thousands of years; but the rapid decline in the magnetic field is already damaging satellites.

The European Union has decided to take on the challenge of saving the world, approving the deployment of a trio of new satellites, called "Swarm." The mission of "Swarm" is to monitor the collapsing field; helping scientists forecast when the compass needles will start pointing south.

"We want to get some idea of how this would evolve in the near future, just like people trying to predict the weather," said French geophysicist Gauthier Hulot. "I'm personally quite convinced we should be able to work out the first predictions by the end of the mission."

To better understand the magnetic field collapse, the European Space Agency plans to launch the three satellites in 2009. The spacecraft, flying in polar orbits a few hundred miles up, are to map its intricacies until perhaps 2015.

Dr. Hulot said scientists would combine the satellite data with computer simulations to make not only distant forecasts but possible warnings of current hazards.

Some experts suggest a magnetic field reversal is overdue. "The fact that it's dropping so rapidly gives you pause," said Dr. John A. Tarduno, a professor of geophysics at the University of Rochester.

Will the Toilets Flush Backwards?

Here's how the magnetic field works: Deep inside the Earth, the magnetic field arises as its fluid core oozes with hot currents of molten iron. This mechanical energy gets converted into electromagnetism.

This process is known as the "geodynamo." In a car's generator, the same principle turns mechanical energy into electricity. The Earth's magnetic field helps shield the planet from solar winds and deadly particle storms. This protective shield, the *magnetosphere*, extends out 37,000 miles from Earth's sunlit side and much farther behind the planet, forming a comet-like tail.

A weak magnetic field could allow solar storms to pummel the atmosphere with enough radiation to destroy significant amounts of the ozone layer. The ozone layer protects the Earth from harmful ultraviolet radiation, short, invisible rays from the sun, that can harm some life forms, depress crop yields and increase cancer rates and cataracts in humans.

News of the current field collapse drew wide scientific attention on April 11, 2002, when the British journal *"Nature"* published a paper that detailed its growing weakness. Dr. Hulot and colleagues at the Institut de Physique du Globe de Paris, as well as the Danish Space Research Institute, called the large drop in magnetism "remarkable."

Spots Before Our Eyes

The sun storm "season" is an established science. An eleven-year cycle of sunspot activity emerges from the detailed records of the twenty-one sunspot cycles that have been observed by astronomers since 1755. Since 2000, solar flares, or sun spots, have been steadily increasing in both frequency and intensity.

This is how *Space.com* described the first solar storms of 2003:

> During late October and early November of 2003, 10 powerful solar flares kicked up extreme doses of X-

rays and other radiation, along with slower-moving storms of charged particles. One flare was by far the most powerful ever measured.[8]

All the eruptions were spawned by huge, magnetically unstable sunspots during a two-week stretch of heightened solar activity unlike anything on record. Mars, unlike the Earth, has no magnetosphere. As a consequence, a substantial part of Mars upper atmosphere was sucked into space by the solar storms.

In September, 2005, a series of solar flares created another disruptive solar storm that bathed the upper atmosphere with radiation so intense that aircraft were diverted north to shield them from the full force of the blast.

Another series in late 2006 created a cosmic storm so fierce it forced the space shuttle to seek cover behind a specially shielded section of the international space station.

"The radio Sun is even brighter now than it was in 2000," David Hathaway, a solar physicist at the NASA Marshall Space Flight Center, said in an interview on NASA's website. By the radio standard, this second peak is larger than the first, noted NASA.

What is particularly fascinating is that a pattern of unusual solar activity is emerging; dating to about 1948. as noted by Phillip F. Schewe, Ben Stein, and James Riordon of the American Institute of Physics.

They noted:

> In the case of sunspots, the direct counting goes back to Galileo's time, around 1610. But earlier sunspot activity can be deduced from beryllium-10 traces in Greenland and Antarctic ice cores.[9]

Using this approach, scientists at the University of Oulu in Finland and the Max Planck Institute in Katlenburg-Lindau in Germany have reconstructed the sunspot count back to the year 850.

They reached the stunning conclusion that, over the whole 1150 year record available, the sun has been most magnetically active (greatest number of sunspots) during the past six decades than at anytime in more than a thousand years.

Why is this important? Taken together with other signs from nature, one gets the image of a planet in upheaval.

"The Sky is Falling"

The 2004 Asian tsunami was triggered by an undersea earthquake of such force that it shook the whole planet like a tuning fork, tipping it slightly on its axis and making microscopic changes in the fabric of time. The island of Sumatra was displaced from its original position by the quake.

Environmental scientists warn of both catastrophic global warming and the approach of a new Ice Age.

Everything from man-made greenhouse gases, to changes in the earth's magnetic field, to cow flatulence is being blamed for the rapidly changing environment. The only thing everybody can agree on is that the environment is rapidly changing. More disasters – natural and unnatural – were reported in 2000 than in any year in the preceding decade.

On average, natural disasters - not man-made ones - accounted for eighty-eight percent of all deaths from disasters from 1990-2000.

While the number of geophysical disasters has remained fairly steady, the number of hydro-meteorological disasters since 1996 has more than doubled. 2004's Hurricane Katrina was the 4th most powerful storm to ever strike the United States and arguably was the single most destructive storm in history. It is the only storm on record to kill a major US city.

The Munich Insurance Group reported that; "...in 1999 at least 70,000 people were killed by natural catastrophes and perhaps even as many as 100,000." It notes somberly:

> This is the highest figure since 1991.... Earthquakes in August and November claimed more than 20,000 lives in Turkey. Cyclone 05 B, which raged in the Bay of Bengal at the end of October, killed as many as 30,000 in Orissa (India). The death toll in Venezuela probably exceeded 30,000 as a result of debris avalanches and mudslides following torrential rain.[10]

The December 26, 2004 tsunami that struck southern Asia killed so many hundreds of thousands of people that the exact number may never be known.

Earthquakes Famines and Wars

Two thousand years ago, "... as He sat upon the Mount of Olives, His disciples came unto Him privately ..." Peter, James, John and Andrew were among Jesus' questioners.

Before moving on, take note of two things;

First, Jesus was speaking with His closest confidantes. Secondly, they were not Christians, but Jews. The Church had not yet been born at Pentecost. The perspective, therefore, is that of Israel, specifically, the view from the Mount of Olives.

Jesus spoke of "wars and commotions" wherein:

> Nation shall rise against nation, and kingdom against
> kingdom: And great earthquakes shall be in divers
> places, and famines, and pestilences; and fearful sights
> and great signs shall there be from heaven.
>
> (Luke 21:9-11)

From our various vantage points around the globe, we *hear*
of ethnic wars, but Israel has spent its entire existence
fighting exactly that. *Ethnic* wars against Arabs in general,
together with specific wars against literal Arab kingdoms.

Jesus said that:

> Before all these, they shall lay their hands on you, and
> persecute you, delivering you up to the synagogues,
> and into prisons, being brought before kings and rulers
> for My Name's sake.
>
> (Luke 21:12)

Israel's rebirth was a direct result of the Nazi Holocaust
during which Jews were exterminated in the millions as
"Christ-killers" by a largely Catholic Europe.

The prophetic pattern outlined for the last days then shifts
from man-made disasters to natural disasters;

> And there shall be signs in the sun, and in the moon,
> and in the stars; and upon the earth distress of nations,
> with perplexity; the sea and the waves roaring.

Weigh the Lord's prophecy against the scientific warnings
of shifting weather patterns, increased flooding, sunspots,
unprecedented hurricane activity, and the literally billions
of dollars being spent to study the existential threats facing
the planet, from a coming global ice age to the possibility
of a catastrophic meteor strike.

The Last Generation

"Men's hearts failing them for fear, and for looking after those things which are coming on the earth: for the powers of heaven shall be shaken" (Luke 21:26).

Think this through. Has there ever been a time - in all recorded history - when the statement above has been truer than in the present generation?

Was there ever a time in all recorded history when *so many* people were aware of the threat of global catastrophe as there are now?

Think of some time - in all recorded history - when it would be accurate to describe the planetary mood as one in which *men's hearts* could be described as *failing them for fear* - not as a result of some temporary man-made event, such as World War Two, but out of fear of *what is coming on the earth* - as a direct result of *the powers of heaven (being) shaken* in such a direct and obvious way?

First we have the climactic upheaval, followed by fears of existential threats from terrestrial and extraterrestrial sources.

Jesus laid out the scenario in chronological order, and historical hindsight enables us to track the progression, from its convergence point in history with the rebirth of Israel to the present (where we sit on the future/historical curve at this moment).

Jesus then turns His attention from future events to explain, in context, what it all means; from the perspective of the generation that would witness all these things ....

"And when these things *begin to come to pass*, then look up, and lift up your heads; for your redemption draweth nigh" (Luke 21:28).[11]

Finally, we have the Lord's ironclad promise: "Verily I say unto you, *this* generation shall *not pass away*, till *all* be fulfilled" (Luke 21:32)[12]

CHAPTER EIGHT

THE REVIVED ROMAN EMPIRE

> And after threescore and two weeks shall Messiah be
> cut off, but not for himself: and the people of the
> prince that shall come shall destroy the city and the
> sanctuary; and the end thereof shall be with a flood,
> and unto the end of the war desolations are
> determined.
>
> (Daniel 9:26)

In 586 B.C., the Southern Kingdom of Judah fell to King
Nebuchadnezzar of Babylon. The ancient city-state was
located some 56 miles south of Baghdad in modern Iraq.
Following the practice of the times, the Babylonians
deported the best and brightest from Jerusalem to Babylon.

In 722 B.C., Sargon the Assyrian had done the same thing
with the ten Northern Tribes when he conquered the
Kingdom of Israel. The ten Northern tribes were uprooted
and relocated elsewhere in the Assyrian Empire.

The purpose was simple. Mass deportation was the most
effective way of preventing popular insurrections. A
conquered people might fight to regain their own land, so
that connection between the people and the land was
severed. The practice resulted in the famed *Ten Lost Tribes*
of Israel.

Nebuchadnezzar practiced a modified form of this kind of
pacification. Deporting an entire population was difficult,

expensive and dangerous. Instead he ordered some ten thousand of Judah's leading citizens, including the king and his court, taken captive and relocated to Babylon.

While Sargon deported the entire population of the Kingdom of Israel, Nebuchadnezzar only deported the most prominent citizens of Judah: professionals, priests, craftsmen, and the wealthy.

Among the estimated ten thousand prominent Jews deported to Babylon was a Jewish teenager named Daniel, which means, *God is my judge.* It is unclear exactly what station Daniel held in Judah before the exile that merited his deportation, but tradition suggests he was a member of Judah's upper-class, and possibly a member of the royal family.

Daniel entered government service as a member of the magi, traditionally a hereditary priesthood who used astrology to advise the king. The magi served in a triune capacity; they were both religious leaders and civil servants who offered political counsel to the King.

The King's Dream

While Daniel was a young man, King Nebuchadnezzar had a dream that greatly troubled him. When he awoke, Nebuchadnezzar summoned his counselors to interpret the dream for him.

Nebuchadnezzar, like many kings of antiquity, was accustomed to consulting astrologers and magicians, especially for the interpretation of dreams.

But this time, his demand was extremely unusual because he was asking more than an interpretation of the dream; the king wanted to know everything about the dream including all that he saw in it. Making things more difficult for the magi, the king had completely forgotten the subject of the dream.

> Then spake the Chaldeans to the king in Syriack, O king, live for ever: tell thy servants the dream, and we will shew the interpretation. The king answered and said to the Chaldeans, The thing is gone from me: if ye will not make known unto me the dream, with the interpretation thereof, ye shall be cut in pieces, and your houses shall be made a dunghill.
>
> (Daniel 2:4-5)

Of course, the astrologers were unable to comply, and when they told this to the king, he became furious and ordered the destruction of his entire corps of counselors. Daniel was arrested along with the others.

"And the decree went forth that the wise men should be slain; and they sought Daniel and his fellows to be slain" (Daniel 2:13).

Daniel went to the king to plead for time, promising that he would consult his God and assured the king that he would not only relate the king's dream back to him, but would also tell him what the dream meant.

After enlisting his Hebrew companions, Hananiah, Mishael, and Azariah to join him in prayer, Daniel returned to the king:

> Daniel answered in the presence of the king, and said, The secret which the king hath demanded cannot the wise men, the astrologers, the magicians, the soothsayers, shew unto the king; But there is a God in heaven that revealeth secrets, and maketh known to the king Nebuchadnezzar what shall be in the latter days.
>
> (Daniel 2:27-28a)

Daniel told the king that, in his dream, he had seen a great image of a man with a head of gold. The breast and arms of the image were of silver; its belly and thighs were of brass, with two legs of iron, while its feet were a mixture of iron and "miry clay" (Daniel 2:33). Then, said Daniel:

> Thou sawest till that a stone was cut out without hands, which smote the image upon his feet that were of iron and clay, and brake them to pieces.
>
> Then was the iron, the clay, the brass, the silver, and the gold, broken to pieces together, and became like the chaff of the summer threshingfloors; and the wind carried them away, that no place was found for them: and the stone that smote the image became a great mountain, and filled the whole earth.
>
> (Daniel 2:34-35)

As Daniel related back the dream to Nebuchadnezzar, the king was astonished, confirming the dream and demanding to know what it meant.

Daniel told the king that the image represented four coming world empires. The head of gold, Daniel told the king, was his own kingdom of Babylon. Daniel predicted Nebuchadnezzar's kingdom would be replaced by an inferior kingdom, represented by the chest and arms of silver.

This inferior kingdom would in turn be replaced by a third world empire, represented by the belly and thighs of brass. That kingdom would be replaced by the two legs of iron. The fourth and final kingdom was represented by the feet of clay, made out of iron mixed with clay, which Daniel interpreted as meaning that final kingdom would be partly strong and partly weak.

> And as the toes of the feet were part of iron, and part of clay, so the kingdom shall be partly strong, and

partly broken. And whereas thou sawest iron mixed with miry clay, they shall mingle themselves with the seed of men: but they shall not cleave one to another, even as iron is not mixed with clay.

(Daniel 2: 42-43)

Daniel said the ten toes of the image represented ten kings who would together rule this last global empire, until that kingdom would be destroyed by God Himself.

And whereas thou sawest the feet and toes, part of potters' clay, and part of iron, the kingdom shall be divided; but there shall be in it of the strength of the iron, forasmuch as thou sawest the iron mixed with miry clay.

(Daniel 2:41)

Did you notice? The dream that Daniel interpreted did not foretell a fifth global/universal kingdom to follow after the fourth, but rather the division of the fourth kingdom - Rome.

Forasmuch as thou sawest that the stone was cut out of the mountain without hands, and that it brake in pieces the iron, the brass, the clay, the silver, and the gold; the great God hath made known to the king what shall come to pass hereafter: and the dream is certain, and the interpretation thereof sure.

(Daniel 2:45)

Future History from the Distant Past

History records the accuracy of Daniel's interpretation. Babylon (the head of gold) was conquered by the Medo-Persian Empire (chest and arms of silver). The Persian Empire succumbed to the Greek Empire of Alexander the Great (belly and thighs of brass). Alexander's Greece was replaced by what became the Roman Empire (two legs of iron).

Eventually, the Roman Empire grew too large to be administered from Rome and split into two parts. The Western Roman Empire continued to be ruled from Rome, while the Eastern Empire was headquartered in Constantinople (modern Ankara, Turkey).

But what of the final empire represented by the feet and toes of iron mixed with clay?

In the third century, the Roman Emperor Constantine declared Christianity to be the state religion of the Roman Empire and declared himself pontiff, or pope. The great historian Edward Gibbons argued in his *Rise and Fall of the Roman Empire* that Rome's empire fell to the Goths and Vandals sometime around A.D. 476.

It was something of an arbitrary date; some argue it took another hundred years before the Roman Empire was no more. But the Roman Empire's demise was unique in one respect. Rome never *fell*. It collapsed under its own weight. The previous empires of Babylon, Persia and Greece were conquered from the outside and absorbed into the conquering empires.

Rome was never actually conquered, and while the empire collapsed, its political influence remained throughout the centuries through the institution set up by Constantine.

Throughout European history and until relatively recently, no European monarch could ascend his throne without the blessing and acquiescence of the Vatican. In medieval times, the Vatican had its own army, and the Popes were not shy about deploying it against European kings who did not bow to their authority.

Within their homelands, European kings relied on Vatican-appointed bishops to help govern their kingdoms. Bishops were involved in castle building, warfare, acted as ambassadors to foreign countries and financial advisors.

The French Revolution was fought, at least in part, to depose Papal influence in France. In 1764, the French expelled the Order of the Jesuits, who served the Vatican as a kind of secret intelligence service.

The famously secular government set up following the French Revolution was so designed to prevent the Vatican from regaining influence over the French government.

After political Rome collapsed, it was replaced by the "Holy Roman Empire" that embraced most of Europe and Italy under the German kings who ruled from 962 to 1806.

It was considered to be a restoration and continuation of the ancient Roman Empire, although in fact it had little in common with its predecessor. Earlier, the Frankish king Charlemagne had revived the same name. His Roman Empire lasted from 800 to 925. In 962, Otto I of Germany and Pope John XII cooperated in a second revival.

Threatened in his possession of the Papal States by Berengar II, king of Italy, John begged Otto to come to his aid. Otto did so, and the pope solemnly crowned him Emperor of the Romans as a reward. From this time, the German kings claimed the right to rule the empire.

This view of the relationship between church and state, which dated from the reign of Roman emperor Constantine, was generally accepted by both emperors and Popes throughout the history of Europe until the end of the 17th century.

After the Treaty of Westphalia (1648) the Holy Roman Empire was little more than a loose confederation of about

300 independent principalities and 1,500 or more semi-sovereign bodies or individuals.

Napoleon I finally destroyed the empire. After defeating Austria and its imperial allies in 1797 and 1801, he annexed parts of Germany and suggested that the larger territories compensate themselves by confiscating the free cities and ecclesiastical states.

On March 6, 1806, under pressure from Napoleon, Francis II abdicated his seat as the Holy Roman Emperor and declared the old empire dissolved.

As the prophet Daniel had foretold, Imperial Rome's "two legs of iron" buckled, but the feet of iron and clay continued to leave their footprints across European history.

The Beast that Was, is Not and Yet is

According to the Prophet Daniel, the final form of world government will be headed by the prince of the people who destroyed Jerusalem and the Temple following the "cutting off" of the Messiah" (Daniel 9:26).

In A.D. 70, weary of constant rebellion in the Roman province of Judea, Roman legions under the command of future Emperor Titus put down the insurrection once and for all. The Roman legions marched on Jerusalem, slaughtering Jews wholesale until there were no longer enough left to mount any kind of serious rebellion.

The Roman historian Flavius Josephus, an eyewitness, recorded the slaughter, writing that some places in Jerusalem, the blood was "as deep as a horse's bridle."

Titus ordered the Temple, the center of Jewish society, destroyed and the Jewish inhabitants of Jerusalem sent into exile. He ordered Judea renamed *Palestina* to further disassociate the Jews from their ancient homeland.

When the Romans set fire to the Temple, its rich ornate gold fixtures melted and ran between the cracks of the stone blocks from which the Temple was constructed. To retrieve this prize, Roman soldiers literally dismantled the Temple, block by block, until all that remained was the retaining wall of the First Temple destroyed 700 years earlier by Nebuchadnezzar.

According to Daniel, the feet and toes of clay belonging to Nebuchadnezzar's image, the "ten kings" whose kingdoms will be partly strong and partly weak would be the final form of a revived political Roman Empire.

Mystery Babylon

The Apostle John divided this final empire into two divisions, political Rome, and religious Rome.

"And the beast that was, and is not, even he is the eighth, and is of the seven, and goeth into perdition." John was also given a vision of ten kings, similar to Daniel's description of revived Rome. "And the ten horns which thou sawest are ten kings, which have received no kingdom as yet; but receive power as kings one hour with the beast" (Revelation 17:11-12).

Revelation identifies the *beast* as a kind of unholy trinity. The *beast* is a religious system.

> And there came one of the seven angels which had the seven vials, and talked with me, saying unto me, Come hither; I will shew unto thee the judgment of the great whore that sitteth upon many waters: With whom the kings of the earth have committed fornication, and the inhabitants of the earth have been made drunk with the wine of her fornication. And the woman was arrayed in purple and scarlet colour, and decked with gold and

precious stones and pearls, having a golden cup in her hand full of abominations and filthiness of her fornication:

(Revelation 17:1-4)

This system, John calls "mystery Babylon"; closing the circle that opened with Daniel's Babylon under Nebuchadnezzar.

And upon her forehead was a name written, MYSTERY, BABYLON THE GREAT, THE MOTHER OF HARLOTS AND ABOMINATIONS OF THE EARTH. And I saw the woman drunken with the blood of the saints, and with the blood of the martyrs of Jesus: and when I saw her, I wondered with great admiration.

(Revelation 17:5-6)

Much of Imperial Rome's history was written in the blood of the early Church; those who were martyred by Rome for refusing to reject Jesus and worship Caesar. The history of spiritual Rome is similarly bloodstained. As we've already seen, the Vatican did not only *commit fornication with the kings of the earth* during the Dark Ages; John also pictures her as drunk with the blood of the martyrs.

During the Inquisition, millions of Christians were martyred by agents of the Vatican. _Foxe's Book of Martyrs_ provides an eyewitness account of the Papal slaughter of Christians, including John Wycliffe, whose crime was to print the Bible in the common language. It is reported that he was burned at the stake, atop a bonfire of burning Bibles.

"And here is the mind which hath wisdom. The seven heads are seven mountains, on which the woman sitteth" (Revelation 17:9).

The city of Rome is known as the *City on Seven Hills*. It is the only city that is also the seat of a religious system whose history conforms perfectly to John's description of the religious system, "Mystery Babylon."

Out of that system, John says, will arise ten kings:

> ...which have received no kingdom as yet; but receive power as kings one hour with the beast. These have one mind, and shall give their power and strength unto the beast.
>
> (Revelation 17:11-12).

The Political Beast

> And I stood upon the sand of the sea, and saw a beast rise up out of the sea, having seven heads and ten horns, and upon his horns ten crowns, and upon his heads the name of blasphemy. And the beast which I saw was like unto a leopard, and his feet were as the feet of a bear, and his mouth as the mouth of a lion: and the dragon gave him his power, and his seat, and great authority.
>
> (Revelation 13:1-2)

The political beast that "rises out of the sea" (of nations) is the Roman prince of Daniel 9:26 – a personality popularly dubbed *the antichrist*. John describes the beast using the same symbology employed by Daniel, who identified each future empire with the image of an animal.

> And four great beasts came up from the sea, diverse one from another. The first was like a lion, and had eagle's wings: I beheld till the wings thereof were plucked, and it was lifted up from the earth, and made stand upon the feet as a man, and a man's heart was given to it.
>
> And behold another beast, a second, like to a bear, and

173

it raised up itself on one side, and it had three ribs in the mouth of it between the teeth of it: and they said thus unto it, Arise, devour much flesh.

After this I saw in the night visions, and behold a fourth beast, dreadful and terrible, and strong exceedingly; and it had great iron teeth: it devoured and brake in pieces, and stamped the residue with the feet of it: and it was diverse from all the beasts that were before it; and it had ten horns.

(Daniel 7: 3-7)

John's *beast* is represented by the same four beasts of Daniel's vision; a leopard, a bear, and a fourth beast John says is energized by the dragon (Satan). Clearly, the symbolism suggests that the empire of The Beast will include all the empires that came before.

John's fourth, (political) Beast, like the Caesars of the early Church, will demand to be worshipped as if he were a god.

And they worshipped the dragon which gave power unto the beast: and they worshipped the beast, saying, Who is like unto the beast? who is able to make war with him? ... And all that dwell upon the earth shall worship him, whose names are not written in the book of life of the Lamb slain from the foundation of the world.

(Revelation 13:4, 8)

The Religious "Beast"

The third member of this coming unholy trinity is known as the false prophet.

"And I beheld another beast coming up out of the earth; and he had two horns like a lamb, and he spake as a dragon" (Revelation 13:11).

The political Beast rises up out of the sea (of nations), but the religious Beast is pictured as arising out of "the earth." The word translated *earth* is a form of the Greek word, *ge* and can mean either "the earth" in general, or "a country, land enclosed within fixed boundaries, a tract of land, territory, region."

Many great Bible expositors have concluded that this refers to the religious Beast arising out of the Land of Israel. Since Israel is included among the nations under the antichrist's rule, it seems logical for the False Prophet to have Jewish roots, since the Jews initially embrace him, despite the fact he has "two horns like a lamb" – symbolizing a counterfeit form of Christianity.

In any case, John clearly identifies the source of his religious power as emanating from "the Dragon" (Satan). We'll discuss this in greater detail in a future chapter. At the moment, we'll continue to address the incredible revival of the old Roman Empire in this generation.

The Benelux Treaty

After two attempts in one century to reunite Europe by force, the aftermath of World War II brought about the unexpected, but necessary economic union of Europe to rebuild the rubble left over by the carnage of war.

The 1948 Benelux Treaty resulted in the establishment of the Western European Union (WEU). With the signing in Brussels of the Treaty of Mutual Assistance of the Western Union [United Kingdom, Benelux (Belgium, The Netherlands, and Luxembourg as a group) and France] Europe began to come together in the name of peace, not conquest.

The 1948 Benelux Treaty led to the 1949 creation of the Council of Europe which in its turn led to the expansion of the Benelux Treaty under the terms of the 1957 Treaty of Rome which led to the Western European Union.

Eventually, the Western European Union grew to ten nations. The Maastricht Treaty in 1993 created the European Union. The EU grew out of the original ten members of the Western European Union as associate members. The original ten became known as Assembly of the Western European Union. Here's a thumbnail sketch of WEU history:

> On the initiative of the Belgian and French Governments, a preliminary joint meeting of the Foreign and Defence Ministers within the WEU framework was held in Rome on 26 and 27 October 1984. It was marked by the adoption of the founding text of WEU's reactivation: the "Rome Declaration." Work on the definition of a European security identity and the gradual harmonisation of its members' defence policies were among the stated objectives. Ministers recognised the "continuing necessity to strengthen western security," and that better utilization of WEU would not only contribute to the security of Western Europe but also to an improvement in the common defence of all the countries of the Atlantic Alliance.
>
> The Rome Declaration reaffirmed that the WEU Council could – pursuant to Article VIII (3) of the modified Brussels Treaty – consider the implications for Europe of crises in other regions of the world.
>
> Pursuant to the decisions taken in Rome, the WEU Council was henceforth to hold two meetings a year at Ministerial level, in which Foreign and Defence Ministers were to sit at the same conference table. [1]

So we have the military arm of Europe - the real power - resting with the ten nation WEU, under the authority of the Rome Declaration.

This revived Roman Empire that now covers all of Europe came into being by peaceful means after centuries of war. Europe's vision of "peace" in the Middle East involves the creation an anti-Israeli terrorist state next door to Israel. Daniel 8:25 predicted the method by which the antichrist's government will come into being saying, "by peace (he) shall destroy many."

Coincidences Abound

The 1948 Benelux Treaty was followed by the 1957 Treaty of Rome, and eventually by the Maastricht Treaty that its supporters hailed as the "revival of the old Roman Empire."

The simultaneous restoration of both Israel and a European Empire corresponding to that of Imperial Rome must now fall into the *coincidence* category.

The Apostle John prophesied that the antichrist will preside over a centralized, global economy so tightly controlled that he would be able to restrict *all* buying and selling to those who worship him. From John's day until 1948, such control was technically impossible.

Impossible, that is, until Bell Labs invented the transistor, giving birth to the Computer Age in 1948; the same year the UN's General Agreement on Tariffs and Trade globalized the world's leading economies. The present World Trade Organization was created to replace GATT, truly globalizing the economy under a single authority. *Coincidence?*

John writes that eventually the whole world will come under the sway of a single religious authority. The World Council on Religions, a UN *Non-Government Organization* that embraces all religions as equal, was born in Amsterdam in August, 1948. *Coincidence?*

John prophesied of the "kings of the east" a great invading army numbering two hundred million men. Today, that is the approximate strength of the Communist Chinese military, born out of Mao Tse Tung's 1948 Cultural Revolution.

And so it goes. Let's recap the *coincidences* unique to this generation.

Israel was reborn in 1948. The European Community was born out of the Benelux Treaty of 1948.

The Russian/Muslim alliances with Syria, Iran, Iraq, Lebanon and the rest of the Arab world, as well as the US support of Israel were the result of the 1948 Truman Doctrine that gave us the Cold War and set the stage for the fulfillment of Ezekiel's prophecy of the Gog-Magog War. (We'll discuss this in greater detail as we move along)

The Gog Magog Alliance already exists, precisely as Ezekiel outlined it, and is directly rooted in the 1948 outbreak of hostilities between Israel and the Islamic world.

That is a lot of *coincidences.*

The Big Picture

Bible prophecy's *Big Picture* was, until 1948, like a jig-saw puzzle still in the box. All the pieces existed to make the picture, but until some of them started coming together, none of them made sense on their own.

Putting a jigsaw puzzle together, you start with the edges, since they are the easiest to identify. From there, you work inward. As this generation progressed, a few puzzle pieces began to fit here, a few more there, but most of the pieces were still in the box.

And, like a jigsaw puzzle, as the *Big Picture* began to take shape, the rest of the pieces became easier to connect. In 1948, the edges were done.

A few pieces were added in the 1970's when Yasser Arafat introduced the West to Islamic terror. A few more with the 1990 collapse of the Soviet Union. A few more fit following the seven-year Oslo Agreement signed in 1993.

But the Big Picture really began taking shape as we entered the 21st century, when an attack on the seat of both the global government and global economy launched a global war between religions.

The aftermath of the attack laid bare old animosities, created new alliances, and reshaped the global geopolitical system in the space of less than five years.

The post-2000 political civil war in the United States filled in another puzzle piece. How could a nation as sophisticated as the United States ever fall victim to the kind of delusion the Bible describes as overtaking the whole world?

A quick perusal of the New York Times or a half hour of CNN dispels that question. If not, then history of the 21st century so far should fill in remaining any blank spots.

According to the Bible, in the last days, the most important country on earth will be Israel. The most important city on earth will be Jerusalem. Given that the world is about to be plunged into global war over the existence of Israel and her possession of Jerusalem, it is hard to dispute that assessment.

The Last Generation

The Bible says revived Israel will live in a state of war until a leader from the revived Roman Empire confirms a seven year peace treaty - predicated on the principle of land for peace.

> Thus shall he do in the most strong holds with a strange god, whom he shall acknowledge and increase with glory: and he shall cause them to rule over many, and shall *divide the land for gain.*

(Daniel 11:39)

What Are The Odds?

Ask yourself a question: What are the odds? Daniel identified, in advance, the four successive world empires of human civilization. Daniel said there would only be four. History says there *were* only four.

Daniel and John both predicted the final world empire's seeming collapse, and foresaw its continued influence throughout history, and foretold its eventual revival, right down to its composition in the last days.

Daniel said it would revive, but would not "cleave" together well, like iron mixed with clay, and would be partly strong and partly weak. The modern European Union exists, despite grave and fundamental differences among its members, as a democratic union. Democracies are, by definition, partly strong and partly weak.

The most powerful democracy the world has ever known is the United States. America is not an empire, however. It is a superpower, but it hasn't the territorial ambitions necessary for empires.

No nation on earth could stand against America in a head to head fight. But America's political democracy was not strong enough to defeat the Iraqi insurgency, because of the political climate at home.

America was no less powerful thirty years ago. But the politics of democracy prevented America from prevailing in Vietnam, a war history shows America won on the battlefield but lost in the ballot box. Describing a democracy as "partly strong and partly weak, like iron mixed with clay," is the *perfect* description.

Not only did both Daniel and John say that the fourth empire would be revived in the last days, they would do so at a time when there was once again a nation on the earth known as Israel.

As we have seen, there has been no nation on earth called "Israel" since Sargon the Assyrian destroyed it more than 2700 years ago. And no political entity resembling the Roman Empire has existed on the earth since the 4th century A.D..

In this generation, both exist. Both are revived forms of their previous historical incarnations. Both lay dormant for millennia, until exactly the same moment in history. Israel declared her existence in May, 1948

The political Roman Empire began its revival with the Benelux Treaty of 1948 that led to the Treaty of Rome which in turn led to the modern European super-state.

The Apostle John described "Mystery Babylon" using the symbols of a woman, riding up a scarlet colored beast. Europe's own chosen symbol is that of the woman, Europa, astride Minos, a mythological beast.

These *coincidences* are just the tip of the iceberg – there are more similarities between *Mystery Babylon* and the *EU* than we can list in a single chapter. But taking just these few, ask yourself: What are the odds?

CHAPTER NINE

GLOBAL ECONOMY

The History of Money

> For the love of money is the root of all evil: which while some coveted after, they have erred from the faith, and pierced themselves through with many sorrows.
>
> (I Timothy 6:10)

Before going on, let me first point out that the Apostle identified the *love* of money, not money itself, as the root of all evil. Money is neither good nor evil.

Money has been around in some form since ancient times. In ancient Egypt and Greece, grain was often used as money. But making a purchase with hundred pound sacks of grain necessarily limited the amount of change you could carry around for casual purposes. And you couldn't very well put away a little for a rainy day. By then, it was likely to be penicillin.

So a more durable substitute was necessary. Ultimately, gold became the preferred medium of exchange. It was rare, durable, and useful both for what could be made from it, and for its intrinsic beauty.

Gold coins were easy to stamp, and impossible to counterfeit. After all, what good is a counterfeit currency that is worth as much as the legitimate variety? Gold was the perfect choice. Silver was a little less rare, and a little less beautiful, but still a highly prized metal.

Soon most coins were minted from one of the two precious metals. By medieval times storing gold and silver coins was becoming a major headache for the average citizen. In addition to its other merits, gold and silver was untraceable. So keeping a lot of coins around the old mud shack was an invitation to thieves.

The local goldsmith generally had the most secure facilities and the means to hire mercenaries to guard his establishment when necessary. It became common practice, especially in Britain, to take gold or silver to the goldsmith for safekeeping. He would accept it on deposit, and give the owner a receipt.

The receipts were as "good as gold" and soon people were buying land or merchandise, using the receipts issued them by the goldsmith as payment.

The Birth of Fractional Reserve Banking

The goldsmith noticed something one day that forever changed the face of commerce. At any given time, there was more gold on deposit than there were people surrendering receipts.

This gave him an idea. Even if he issued more receipts than there was gold to redeem them, nobody would ever know; unless everybody showed up to demand their gold at once. But there was little chance of that; so long as nobody suspected their receipts might not be honored.

So the goldsmith began to *lend* money by issuing receipts for gold he didn't have - and charging interest! In so doing, he created *money out of nothing*. The original loan was created out of thin air and the interest was collected against the debtor's future earnings.

Generally, the *loan* was secured by taking a mortgage against collateral - usually real estate. If the creditor repaid the loan, the goldsmith destroyed the phony receipt and pocketed the interest. If the creditor defaulted, the goldsmith would take the collateral property. •

By putting the original amount of the loan back into deposit (if necessary) the goldsmith seized the property. Soon he became a rich man. As his wealth grew, he could afford to issue more bogus receipts and use the seized properties as collateral in the unlikely event more receipts would be issued for payment than there was gold in the vault.

It was a calculated risk, and those goldsmiths who got too greedy often found themselves decorating a tree limb on the edge of town. By and large, however, the scheme worked and the basis for the modern fractional reserve banking was born - the practice of creating money out of thin air!

Fractional reserve banking makes possible two modern economic phenomena, the inflation/deflation cycle and bank failures.

Two Views of History

In the final analysis, there can really only be two possible theories capable of explaining human history. The first and most widely accepted is the *accidental history theory*.

Proponents of *accidental history theory* maintain that things *just happen*. An obscure relative of a Prussian emperor is assassinated in Sarajevo. Then, World War I just happens. The Versailles Treaty that ended the war all but guaranteed future hostilities with Germany.

Accidental history theory has two problems here. First, it insists that nobody could have predicted the effects of the Versailles Treaty on future European peace. Lord Curzon of England, however, said of the treaty; "This is no peace. This is only a truce for twenty years."

Economist John Maynard Keynes was a member of the British delegation at the time of the Treaty. He had this to say: "This peace is outrageous and impossible, and can bring nothing but misfortune behind it." That the Versailles Treaty would fail was hardly unpredictable.

A second problem for the *accidental theory* is that it is not backed up by historical fact. As a matter of historical record, Versailles was indeed a major factor in the outbreak of World War II; proving that the results of Versailles could be predicted, and therefore, by definition, no accident.

An *accidental* view of history would have the United Nations simply come into being in response to the Cold War. According to accidental theory, the Cold War just *happened*. So did its collapse. Clearly, the *accidental history theory* doesn't hold up well under historical scrutiny.

The second view explaining human history is *conspiracy theory*. The *conspiracy theory* of history holds that government doesn't just *happen. Conspiracy theory* views politics as a conspiratorial network of operatives, each championing and attempting to forward a particular agenda over the objections of other politicians whose agendas differ.

Of the two theories, the *accidental theory* seems to be least likely. But, that leaves only one choice - the *conspiracy theory*. People generally don't like the *conspiracy theory*, even though it's the only one that makes sense.

A Word About Conspiracies

"The individual is handicapped by coming face to face with a conspiracy so monstrous he cannot believe it exists" (FBI Director J. Edgar Hoover).

The story of the money trust conspiracy cannot be told without first addressing the issue of conspiracy and conspiracy theories. Conspiracy is not really the right word, but it is the best one we have to describe the shadow government.

The dictionary defines *conspiracy* as; "An agreement to perform together an illegal, wrongful, or subversive act."

Do conspiracies exist? If they do not, than how can we explain communism or Adolf Hitler's Third Reich?

Clearly, conspiracies have existed throughout history; so it is hardly a stretch to consider that some historical conspiracies may survive today. All that is necessary is a sufficiently long-range *Plan*.

The *Plan* can be called a "conspiracy" in the sense it is an agreement together to perform an act. The terms *illegal*, *wrongful* and *subversive,* however, can be subjective. People conspire all the time; with work associates, for example, to advance their position over colleagues.

Politicians constantly conspire to win public favor and personal gain. The CIA MK Ultra mind control program exposed in the late 1970's is another example of a government agency conspiring to implement an agenda the public would not approve. Conspiratorial plots and actions are constantly being exposed.

The investigation into the Clinton White house was a textbook case in conspiracy: conspiracies of silence, cover-up conspiracies, character assassination conspiracies, fall guy conspiracies, witness tampering conspiracies, conspiracies to obstruct justice; just to name the ones we know about.

Conspiracies are a fact of life. If the participants believe their actions to be legal, proper and benevolent toward mankind, are they still "conspirators"?

There are those who scoff at the notion of *secret conspiracies* based on the conventional wisdom that, "nobody could keep a conspiracy secret for generations." It depends on the conspiracy.

What about the Mafia? Rumors existed for years, investigations were conducted, but it took half a century of no-holds-barred investigation and vigorous law enforcement to uncover the existence of *La Cosa Nostra*. And even after Joe Valachi gave his famous testimony, we still only had a vague picture of what the Mafia really was or how it worked.

Imagine, for just a moment, if one combined the long term secrecy of *La Cosa Nostra* with the idea that the *Plan* was noble? Where the ultimate goal wasn't wealth, but instead, utopia, a heaven on earth? Where the ends were so benevolent in scope, so thrilling a gift to humanity, that any means were justified?

History is a tapestry of benevolence and evil; means so inhuman that they seem unjustifiable, except to the *insiders* who see their ends as noble and their means as a form of *tough love.*

Engineered Crises

One of the most enigmatic figures in recent history is also one of the most significant. Paul Warburg was so highly respected a financier that he was tapped by Senator Nelson Aldrich to author a study on discounting commercial bills.

Senator Aldrich, (John D. Rockefeller's father in law), was the chairman of the Senate Finance Committee. In 1910, Aldrich's committee was charged with developing a central banking scheme for the United States, ostensibly to forestall the financial panics that regularly plagued the US economy at the turn of the century.

The United States at that time suffered from periodic liquidity crises, engineered largely by the financial community. Bankers argued that it was due to the rigid nature of the currency supply. In those days, in order to make a loan, the banks actually were required to have the money on deposit!

A system of pyramiding reserve schemes made it possible for banks to obtain further funds, but they could not actually issue loans until those funds became available. Therefore, the bankers argued, adequate money supplies could not be funneled in time to the industries that needed it the most.

Sounds sensible, when you hear the bankers argue it. The argument loses a little weight when you restate the position logically, however. "We want to be able to charge you interest for loans made with money we don't have, so we want you to lend it to us for free first" (via fractional reserve banking).

To ensure the public got the message, a series of currency shortages were engineered. Since the entire banking system was not yet under a central authority, the *panics* were generally localized in predetermined geographic regions across the country.

A large bank, or group of cooperating banks, would restrict credit to farmers and businesses. As a result, businesses were often unable to finance inventories and farmers couldn't pay to get crops to market. Many went under. Such failures had a ripple effect. Grain rotting in the fields meant a shortage of livestock feed. Higher feed prices forced many livestock producers into bankruptcy. Business failures in one industry often weakened other related industries.

Ultimately, the shortage was felt on Wall Street, where market prices would plunge, small, weak banks would fail, and the currency supply would be further restricted. The pressure was on. The destruction of the smaller, weaker banking competitors provided two benefits for those that remained.

One is the obvious - fewer independent banks meant fewer slices of the pie. Secondly, a small number of big banks were much easier to regulate than a larger number of independents. The engineered crises therefore provided a payday on several fronts.

A central banking scheme, argued the bankers, would eliminate financial panics. All that was needed, went the reasoning, was the ability of bankers to lend more money than they had - at interest. Creating money in this way would enable industry to buy now, and pay later when they realized their profits.

Of course, for the scheme to work there must be centralized control of the banking system. The problem, argued the proponents of centralized banking, was that there were just too many rugged individualists in the financial community.

Wise leadership, and absolute control of all banking and monetary policy was necessary to keep these *panics* from repeating themselves.

The Invisible King

Paul Warburg, born in Hamburg in 1868, was the son of a wealthy German banking family who ensured he received the "best" education. At 18, he went straight to London, headquarters of the Rothschild banking empire.

Two years later, sufficiently schooled, he returned to Hamburg where he joined his brothers, Aby and Max, as a partner in the family firm, M.M. Warburg & Company. In 1895, Warburg married Nina Loeb, also the offspring of a Rothschild backed banking dynasty. In 1901, the couple moved to New York. He was immediately offered a partnership in his father in law's firm of Kuhn & Loeb, one of Wall Street's most prestigious firms.

Soon after entering the world of American-style banking, Warburg began to set in motion the plan for a central bank.

Meeting On Jekyll Island

In November 1910, having consulted with Rothschild Banks in England, France, and Germany, Senator Nelson Aldrich boarded a private train in Hoboken, New Jersey. He was headed to a meeting of the world's wealthiest men at a private hunting club owned by J.P. Morgan.

The meeting was to be secret; so secret that even the participants were instructed to address each other by their first names only. Those present represented one-sixth of the world's wealth: Benjamin Strong, President of Morgan's Bankers Trust Company; Charles Norton, President of Morgan's First National Bank of New York; Henry Davidson, senior partner of J. P. Morgan; Frank

Vanderlip, President of Kuhn, Loeb's National City Bank of New York; A. Piatt Andrew, Assistant Secretary of Treasury; and the future Governor of the Federal Reserve, Paul Warburg. Vanderlip later described the meeting as follows:

> There was an occasion near the close of 1910 when I was as secretive, indeed as furtive, as any conspirator. I do not feel it is any exaggeration to speak of our secret expedition to Jekyll Island as the occasion of the actual conception of what eventually became the Federal Reserve System.
>
> We were told to leave our last names behind us. We were told further that we should avoid dining together on the night of our departure. We were instructed to come one at a time... where Senator Aldrich's private car would be in readiness, attached to the rear end of the train for the South.
>
> Once aboard the private car, we began to observe the taboo that had been fixed on last names. Discovery, we knew, simply must not happen, or else all our time and effort would be wasted .... [1]

The goal then, as always, was to devise a central bank scheme that would not suffer the fate of every other effort. The most recent failure was that of the Aldrich Bill of 1910, which proposed something similar to the eventual Federal Reserve, but made the mistake of revealing it as a central bank scheme. As soon as lawmakers heard the words, "central bank" the Aldrich Bill was killed.

Those at the meeting decided that the man to write the new legislative effort at creating a US central bank was Paul Warburg. Senator Aldrich would leave his name off it this time.

Aldrich was adequately compensated for his sacrificed legacy. When he entered the Senate in 1881, his net worth was $50,000. When he left the Senate in 1911, it had risen to $30 million! Politics pays well, if you have the right connections.

Warburg's revised bill was titled "The Federal Reserve Act" to mask its real nature. It proposed to create a system managed by private individuals who would control the nation's issue of money. Furthermore, the Federal Reserve Board, composed of twelve districts and one director (the Federal Reserve Chairman), would control the nation's financial resources by regulating the money supply and available credit; all by mortgaging the government through borrowing.

Who Owns The Fed?

The Federal Reserve is neither "federal" nor a "reserve." It isn't federally owned, and it does not function as a *reserve*. A look at the list of the principle stockholders in the modern Federal Reserve Banking System gives more weight to the term "money trust."

After the Federal Reserve Act was passed into law, six New York banks controlled by the Morgan-Standard Oil Group (J.P. Morgan and John D. Rockefeller) bought controlling interest in the Fed. They have held it ever since. The May 19, 1914 organization chart shows how 88,200 of the original 203,053 shares issued were distributed:

- 30,000 shares - Federal National City Bank *
- 15,000 shares - Morgan-Baker First National Bank*
- 21,000 shares - National Bank of Commerce [Warburg]
- 10,200 shares - Manufacturers Hanover [Rothschild]
- 6000 shares - Chase National Bank

- 6000 shares - Chemical Bank

In 1955, these two banks merged to become Citibank, the retail banking arm of Citicorp.

That gave these six banks 43% of the total shares in the Federal Reserve. By 1983, they controlled 53% of the total stock in the Federal Reserve. This didn't go unnoticed.

The U. S. Senate issued a report June 15, 1978 titled; *"Interlocking Directorates among the Major US Corporations"* looked at who really owned America's largest 130 corporations. These five banks held a total of 470 interlocking directorates, effectively giving them ownership of corporate America as well as the Federal Reserve System. Here's how they broke down, according to the report:

- Citicorp - 97 Directorates

- J. P. Morgan Co - 99 Directorates

- Chemical Bank - 96 Directorates

- Chase Manhattan Bank - 89 Directorates

- Manufacturers Hanover - 89 Directorates

Since the 1978 report, through a series of mergers and acquisitions, these five banks became two: Citicorp and J. P. Morgan Chase. The centralized control this gives means that, in essence, instead of 130 corporations there is really just one, owned by the two banks that are ultimately owned or controlled by the European money trust.

How the Economy Really Works

How our economy works is a mystery to most people, and that is why it so easy to become confused. So confused, in fact, that people actually mount campaigns to repeal tax cuts and raise taxes to "pay off the deficit" - without ever understanding what *paying off the deficit* would mean.

The United States operates on a *deficit* economy; it has ever since the passage of the Federal Reserve Act in 1913 and the confiscation of US gold in 1933. Prior to that, the US had operated as a *barter* economy.

It is the *barter* economy that most Americans believe is in operation today, and that is the fundamental flaw that gives economic and political spin doctors the green light.

In a *barter* economy, something of value is exchanged for something of value. To have value, the thing exchanged must have substance, it must be acceptable in trade for goods and services to the general public, and its supply must be finite - it has to be sufficiently rare as to maintain its value.

The Currency Act of 1793 set the value of American currency as a weight of gold based on a Dutch unit of measure called the "thaler" - a weight we now call a *Troy ounce*. The "thaler" (Americanized as the "dollar") was a unit of measure for a substance of value (gold).

With the confiscation of gold in 1933, the Gold Standard was repealed and replaced by the less-valuable Silver Standard. Suddenly a "thaler" was not a weight of gold, but a weight of silver.

The Federal Reserve began issuing dollar bills called "Silver Certificates" and declared them redeemable in silver. These certificates of weight were replaced in 1963 by the Federal Reserve Note which promised redemption in "Lawful US Money."

The Currency Act of 1793 declared one "thaler" of gold to be "Lawful US Money" - and it has never been repealed by

Congress. When people began demanding redemption of their Federal Reserve Notes in "Lawful US Money" the face of the note was changed to read, "This bill is legal tender" - in effect, declaring a weight of a substance to actually *be* the substance it is supposed to weigh.

This of course was theft; and remains an unpunished theft. It was perpetrated by the money trust controlling the Federal Reserve and made possible the very thing the Fed was ostensibly created to prevent - inflation, deflation, recession and depression.

But it is a fait accompli, and our economy now depends on it. Trying to turn our economy from debit-based back to barter is as possible as turning a pickle back into a cucumber.

A debit-based economy *requires* high deficits to make it work. Investment, production and job growth *depend* on high national debt. Reducing the debt weakens the overall economy.

Life Without Credit...

By way of analogy, let's take a family making about fifty thousand dollars a year. Take that family's credit away; no credit cards, no loans - cash only.

What kind of car can they afford? They would have to save up to buy a new car. What about their housing? How long would it take *you* to save up enough to buy your own home for cash? What about that new fridge? No credit cards, no revolving credit, just cash.

A family making a thousand dollars a week would be just getting by. Suppose we are talking about a family making $100,000 per year - about two thousand dollars per week, and a member of the American "rich"?

What kind of car would *they* drive? It's unlikely it would be new. They could probably save up to buy a house in about ten years; but it would be a starter home. They could buy a new fridge or stove or TV set, but that might put a dent in their home savings account.

Give them back their credit cards, revolving charges, mortgage and car loans, and they are living the American Dream. The family making a hundred thousand dollars a year lives in a nice home in the suburbs, commutes to work in an expensive SUV, and has both new fridges *and* nice retirement savings accounts.

Families making fifty grand a year drive nearly new mini-vans, have nice, but smaller, homes in less expensive neighborhoods and sometimes have to choose between retirement contributions and big-ticket items. But, thanks to a debit-based economy, still live better than they would making twice as much but paying cash for everything.

It is in the interest of the banking and lending institutions to continue lending them money against their accumulated equity because: a) it increases their profits; and b) the collateral is *real* property, whereas the *money* is an illusion - in reality, nothing but a bookkeeping entry.

America's economy *must* be in debt in order to prosper. If you doubt me, look back to when we finally balanced the budget and paid off the national debt in the late 1990's. The economy began to flag and sputter into recession two full quarters before the end of the Clinton administration.

The attacks on 9/11 and the wars in Iraq and against Afghanistan have forced the government to pull its credit cards out of retirement and - Voila! - jobs get created, personal income increases, flagging industries like manufacturing post their best gains in twenty years, and the government starts offering tax cuts (that further reduce any chance of a surplus). The numbers speak for themselves.

An Idea Who's Time Has Come

That's how things work. Learn to live with it. The value of US currency today is based on America's future earnings potential and its collateral assets, just like your credit card limits.

The higher your credit card balances get, the more credit increases you are offered. You then buy more, which creates demand for increased production, which creates demand for new jobs, etc.

On a national level it works the same way. A debit based economy, at its core, is an insidious, evil system that will one day result in a global economic catastrophe. But not yet.

The global economic system based on the same economic model of debit and credit was constructed to a particular purpose. It has taken nearly a century, but it is now in place.

For the first time in human history, thanks to centralized banking, technology and the speed of the internet, it is possible for a single authority to control the world's economic systems. The Bible says that authority will be given to the antichrist in his time, for the purpose of fulfilling Bible prophecy for the last days.

According to Scripture, by the mid-point in the Tribulation, the antichrist's government will have taken the existing, centralized system and turned it into his most powerful weapon. He will combine his control of the economy with his control of the global religious system and will use both to demand worship from those living during that time.

> And he had power to give life unto the image of the beast, that the image of the beast should both speak, and cause that as many as would not worship the image of the beast should be killed. And he causeth all, both small and great, rich and poor, free and bond, to receive a mark in their right hand, or in their foreheads: And that *no man might buy or sell,* save he that had the mark, or the name of the beast, or the number of his name. [2]

(Revelation 13:15-17)

Never before in human history was such a thing possible. The system in place today actually *requires* such control on the national level. The Fed chairman is America's economic supervisor.

A word from him can cause the markets to go up, or go down, or collapse, should he wish it.

For the record, I am *not* identifying the Fed chairman as the antichrist. Every nation in the global economic system has a similar central banking scheme, and a central banker. Control the central bankers (a relative handful of individuals) and the Apostle John's scenario from the book of Revelation would become a reality.

The system stinks. But it is the only one we have and I, for one, am not eager to endure the chaos and catastrophe that would result in trying to change it now.

The Ten-Horned Beast

According to John, the empire of the Beast will have seven heads and ten horns. Currently, the Group of Industrialized Nations consists of Germany, France, Italy, Japan, the UK, the US and Canada.

The Last Generation

After the Soviet Union collapsed, Bill Clinton insisted on bringing Russia to the table as an informal member, and the Group of Seven (G7) became the Group of Eight (G8) as a presidential *thank you* to Russian president Boris Yeltsin.

It was a cosmetic addition - the G7 forms the nucleus of the global economic system. When the G-7 finance ministers come together for their annual meeting, it is formally known as the "G-8 minus Russia."

The economic power remains in the hands of the G-7. Four of the G-7 members are also members of the Western European Union and NATO, so it is no surprise that G-7 economic policy heavily favors the interests of the European Union.

The Apostle John notes that the Beast will seize control of the global economic system and will use its clout to assert and enforce its policies.

Out of that system will arise an individual leader who will be the embodiment of the system of the Beast, in much the same way that Adolf Hitler became the embodiment of the Third Reich.

Recommendation #666

> And he causeth all, both small and great, rich and poor, free and bond, to receive a mark in their right hand, or in their foreheads: And that no man might buy or sell, save he that had the mark, or the name of the beast, or the number of his name.
>
> (Revelation 13:16-17)

In 1999, Javier Solana became the High Representative for the European Union's foreign and security policy, and through *Recommendation #666*, he was given emergency powers over the military wing of the EU in 2000.

Although the WEU is made up of more than 28 countries, there are only ten full members. The rest hold lesser status as either "associate," "observer" or "partner" countries.

Solana's post of uber-boss of both the EU and the WEU was formalized under the authority of the *Recommendation #666*. This has led many to speculate that Solana is the antichrist. Solana heads the system that will become the Beast, but that isn't the same as being the *embodiment* of it.

The prophecy of the Mark of the Beast is one of the most widely known in the Bible. A myriad of fictional books and movies have used it as their plot line. It has launched a particular fascination with what the "number of his name" is and how it fits together.

John writes:

> Here is wisdom. Let him that hath understanding count the number of the beast: for it is the number of a man; and his number is Six hundred threescore and six.
>
> (Revelation 13:18)

The Scripture doesn't identify a *man* as the Beast; it identifies a *system* that is jointly headed by a political and religious leader. John identifies the marriage of the religious system with the political system using the symbol of a woman riding upon a scarlet colored beast.

The engraving on the EU's euro and many of its official documents depict *Europa*, a woman, riding on the back of *Minos*, a beast.

A huge painting of the woman riding the beast hangs in the new EU Parliament building in Brussels. The EU Council of Ministers Office, also in Brussels, greets visitors with a huge sculpture of *Europa* and her *Beast* outside its front entrance.

Mystery Babylon

> So He carried me away in the spirit into the wilderness: and I saw a woman sit upon a scarlet coloured beast, full of names of blasphemy, having seven heads and ten horns. And the woman was arrayed in purple and scarlet colour, and decked with gold and precious stones and pearls, having a golden cup in her hand full of abominations and filthiness of her fornication:
>
> And upon her forehead was a name written, MYSTERY, BABYLON THE GREAT, THE MOTHER OF HARLOTS AND ABOMINATIONS OF THE EARTH. And I saw the woman drunken with the blood of the saints, and with the blood of the martyrs of Jesus: and when I saw her, I wondered with great admiration.

(Revelation 17:3-6)

The woman, the Bible indicates, is a false religion that has joined itself to the political system.

Of the Beast, John was told by the revealing angel:

> The beast that thou sawest was, and is not; and shall ascend out of the bottomless pit, and go into perdition: and they that dwell on the earth shall wonder, whose names were not written in the book of life from the foundation of the world, when they behold the beast that was, and is not, and yet is.

(Revelation 17:8)

The Roman Empire was, and is not, and yet is, in the sense that the Roman Empire was both a religion and a political entity, until political Rome fell. But spiritual Rome endured.

John says that they will merge again in the last days, but only briefly. In the end, the political beast will consume the harlot completely:

> And the ten horns which thou sawest upon the beast, these shall hate the whore, and shall make her desolate and naked, and shall eat her flesh, and burn her with fire.

> (Revelation 17: 16)

John identifies the harlot with "seven mountains, on which the woman sitteth" - a clear indication of Rome, the *City on Seven Hills*; and again as "the woman which thou sawest is that great city, which reigneth over the kings of the earth" (Revelation 17:16, 18).

Within that political system a leader will arise who can be identified, as John says, by the number of a *man*, that number, of course, being 666.

Connecting the Dots

We have a religious system whose history matches that of Papal Rome throughout the Dark Ages, together with a global economic system run by seven heads (G-7) that dictates political and military policy to the ten horns (WEU) whose authority is derived from *Recommendation #666*.

There is no political leader yet, conforming to John's image of the political beast linked to a *man* that is identifiable by "the number of his name" - 666. But there is an empty seat awaiting his arrival.

CHAPTER TEN

THE MARK OF THE BEAST

> And he causeth all, both small and great, rich and poor, free and bond, to receive a mark in their right hand, or in their foreheads: And that no man might buy or sell, save he that had the mark, or the name of the beast, or the number of his name.
>
> (Revelation 13:16-17)

One of the most remarkable examples of Bible prophecy making the leap from the pages of the Bible to the front pages of the daily newspapers is also among the most well-known - the Mark of the Beast.

Now, take a few moments to think about what would be necessary to fulfill this prophecy as written. Keep in mind the fact that the Apostle John penned this prophecy sometime around A.D. 87.

In A.D. 87, literacy was largely limited to members of the upper classes. It was a world in which a person was whom he claimed to be. A person who lived in Asia Minor, for example, could travel a few hundred miles away and become a completely new person.

Say you are a petty thief wanted by the Romans in Judea, so you move to Athens. In Judea, you were Joseph, son of Barnabas. But when you move to Athens, you identify yourself as Dionysius, son of Alexander.

The Last Generation

Unless you run into somebody from your home town in Judea who knows you (an unlikely prospect), you are now Dionysius. Joseph might be wanted by the Romans, but Dionysius has a clean slate.

Who is to say any differently? It isn't like you have to carry an identification card - as already noted, most people couldn't read it if you had one.

But according to the prophecy of the Mark of the Beast, the antichrist would not only be able to positively identify every single person, but would be able to restrict individual freedoms based on their identification.

Sure, there is the "mark" - but the economy of the ancient world was based on the barter system. Currency was whatever the seller would accept in exchange for goods and services.

While it might be possible to hamper an individual's ability to engage in commerce in the big cities, many people in the ancient world lived their entire lives without ever setting foot inside one.

At best, the restrictions described by John would make it more expensive for someone outside the system to buy or sell, human nature and greed dictate that it could never be universally imposed.

For the right price, anybody can buy anything. It is true today, and it was even truer in A.D. 87 when currency was as anonymous and untraceable as the buyers or sellers.

In the modern world, we have strict laws against trafficking in drugs, human slavery, child pornography or stolen merchandise. But if one is willing to pay the price demanded, any or all of the above can be bought.

Even in a literate world like ours where our wallets and purses bulge with different forms of identification, our faces can be identified by biometric scans, our fingerprints are cataloged and the examination of a single hair can not only identify an individual, but can also identify members of an entire family.

If it were not so, there would be no drug cartels, child porn rings or organized crime.

The Impossible Prophecy

In short, the details of John's prophecy were impossible in John's day. It was impossible fifteen hundred years later when Columbus embarked on his voyage of discovery in 1492.

It was even impossible only sixty years ago. Even the Nazis weren't able to round up *every* Jew, or completely eliminate a Jew's ability to buy and sell. Even concentration camp inmates were able to bribe their guards, if they had the wherewithal to do so.

But John's prophecy says "all" and "no man" - and if we are to take the Bible literally, then this prophecy, to be valid, must be literally fulfilled. Even to this moment in history, John's prophecy has not been literally fulfilled.

You cannot open a bank account without satisfactory identification, or make a major purchase using large amounts cash; but small cash transactions are still relatively anonymous.

The proof is that drug dealers, terrorist rings, child porn rings, etc., etc., still exist. For now.

The Last Generation

That window of economic opportunity is slowly closing - and for the first time in history, the technology exists to slam it shut completely.

All that is missing is someone with the political clout and popular support necessary to impose a system such as John describes.

In some cities in the US and, especially in Europe, citizens are already under round-the-clock surveillance by the government. Combining motion detection technology with the learning capabilities of video game software, new surveillance systems can detect people loitering, walking in circles or leaving a package.

New microphone technology can isolate the sound of a gunshot and direct the attached camera to swivel and zoom in on the source. Sensitivity may reach the point where microphones could pick out the word "explosives" spoken in a crowd. Since 9/11, sections of New York, Washington, Los Angeles and Chicago are already under such round-the-clock surveillance.

And in Great Britain, the government has more than 4.2 *million* security cameras trained on its citizens. Each person can be identified by software that can identify someone's face by scanning it and comparing it to public photographic records.

If a photograph of your face has ever been linked to your name, via a driver's license, passport, newspaper clipping, student identification card, etc., then you can be picked out of a crowd, positively identified, and your location pinpointed without your ever knowing it.

Moreover, the implementation of technologies like the *VeriSign* implantable chip has the potential to forever eliminate anonymous economic activity.

Such chips can carry the equivalent of more than 11,000 pages of information about you.

Your name, medical history, driving record, banking records, etc., can be retrieved by simply scanning your chip using the same RFID scanning that Wal-Mart uses to make sure you don't walk out of a store with merchandise you didn't pay for.

Or it can be revoked or flagged as belonging to a "person of interest" - using the same remote RFID technology. Your bank account balance could be zeroed out, or your location could be pinpointed and instantly transmitted to law enforcement.

There are already pilot programs in existence in which purchasers can pay for merchandise by simply walking by a scanner in the story.

The RFID reads the chip on the merchandise, then reads the information on your chip and deducts the price electronically from your bank account. You need only come within range of the scanner.

The technology necessary to fulfill John's prediction never existed until this generation.

The political will and popular support needed to implement this kind of technology didn't exist until the events of first year of the 21st century demonstrated the need to implement it on a universal basis for reasons of public safety and security.

That political will and popular support is by no means universal - yet. Privacy advocacy groups and civil libertarians still oppose it - but public opposition is balanced by the recognition that without it, the events of 9/11 would be repeated over and over.

The Last Generation

It wouldn't take too many more attacks of the magnitude of 9/11 before the public would begin *demanding* some form of universal electronic identification system.

Post 9/11, the most effective tool in the fight against terror has been the effort to cut off funding to the terrorists. Bank transfers, large cash transactions, and all kinds of suspicious financial activity are already being closely monitored.

In August, 2006, two Michigan men of Lebanese descent were charged with money laundering and aiding of terrorism.

The suspects, twenty-year old Osma Sabhi Abulhassan and twenty-year old Ali Houssaiky were residents of Dearborn, Michigan., which is over 300 miles away. The men paid cash for the cell phones and were not required to produce any identification to make the purchases.

Nonetheless, Abulhassan and Houssaiky were pulled over after purchasing 12 disposable cell phones from a local Radio Shack. $11,000 in cash was found in the glove box.

Also found were MapQuest directions for 75 to 100 other Wal-Marts, Radio Shacks and other retailers in Ohio, Kentucky, West Virginia, Virginia, Tennessee, North Carolina and South Carolina.

Since cell-phones are often used by terrorists as remote-control detonation devices, the public breathed a collective sigh of relief and heaped praise on the government's ability to intercept them.

The 666 Mystery

John says the Mark of the Beast can be identified by its connection to the number 666.

Here is wisdom. Let him that hath understanding count
the number of the beast: for it is the number of a man;
and his number is Six hundred threescore and six.

(Revelation 13:18)

Take a look at any barcode - most have numbers printed
below the bars.

Find a barcode that contains the number "6" and locate the
parallel bars that correspond to it. Now look at the three
slightly longer parallel bars that divide the number into
three sections.

Do you see it? Each of these dividers corresponds to the
barcode that represents a "6".

This isn't the Mark of the Beast. Before there can be a
Mark of the Beast, there must first be a beast, and
secondarily, there must be a mark imposed by his system.

But what are the odds that the Apostle John's prophecy of
the Mark of the Beast and link it to computer-sensitivity to
the number 6? Or that it would be used in multiples of 3?

Everything about John's prophecy demands the existence
of a global computer network tied into a global economy
and overseen by a global governmental authority. Until this
generation, it was impossible.

Since September 11, it is inevitable.

Chipping Away...

A few years ago, an American company announced a new
syringe-injectable microchip implant for humans at a
global security conference in Paris. The chip is designed to
be used as a fraud-proof payment method for cash and
credit-card transactions.

The chip is being touted as a defense to identity theft. Identity fraud costs the banking and financial industry some $48 billion a year, and consumers another $5 billion. That is a lot of incentive.

Scott R. Silverman, CEO of Applied Digital Solutions, called the chip a "loss-proof solution" and said that the chip's "unique under-the-skin format" could be used for a variety of identification applications in the security and financial worlds.

Art Kranzley, senior vice president at MasterCard, commented on the *PayPass* system in a *USA Today* interview:

> We're certainly looking at designs like key fobs. It could be in a pen or a pair of earrings. Ultimately, it could be embedded in anything – someday, maybe even under the skin.[1]

That Was Then...

Back in 1992, I covered the *CardTech/SecureTech Conference* held in Washington, DC. The conference was similar to the one being held in Paris, but the technology was in its infancy. The conference attendees included some of the biggest names in banking and technology and the keynote speaker was former CIA Director William Colby.

I was able to interview a number of the attendees, from the then-director of Barclay's Bank in England to the Netherlands smart card guru David Chaum.

There were two central themes to the conference. The first was to be expected - how to get the cost of the chips down (at that time, they were a prohibitively high $5.00 per chip) and, how to get the public to accept the technology by downplaying the *Mark of the Beast* angle (they really called it that in the lectures).

I've said it before - its amazing the difference a decade makes. What was being discussed in 1992 as a theoretical possibility is now reality. A decade ago, the conference attendees were bemoaning the fact many people were uncomfortable with ATM technology.

Now, they bemoan the fact ATM's are insecure. A thief can force someone to disclose their PIN numbers, they argue, and drain the account. An implantable chip, they argue, will prevent that.

This is, of course, nonsense, since most ATM's limit the amount of cash withdrawn in a single day. Back in 1992, the conference attendees were presented with the blueprint for a conditioning process to prepare society for the coming cashless revolution.

First debit cards, then credit card-branded debit cards, then value-added cards, until eventually, cash would become useless except for small purchases.

Ask yourself, how many times have you purchased a big ticket item, like a fridge, or a car, and paid for it in hard cash in the last decade? Today, if you tried to buy a $300 one-way plane ticket for cash, the next person you would meet would be a Homeland Security agent.

The United Religions Zone

"And I beheld another beast coming up out of the earth; and he had two horns like a lamb, and he spake as a dragon" (Revelation 13:11).

Revelation 13 outlines the respective careers of two separate beasts; the political *beast* of Revelation 13:1 and

213

the religious *beast* of Revelation 13:11, the one that John refers to as the *false prophet* (Revelation 16:13, 19:20, 20:10).

The False Prophet is a different person than the antichrist, and, together with their master, Satan, comprise the counterfeit *unholy trinity* of the Tribulation Period.

The antichrist is the political leader who controls the global government and global economy, but the false prophet controls what eventually becomes a compulsory global religious system.

According to Revelation 13:16-18, any person who refuses to accept the *Mark of the Beast*, which is both an act of economic need and one of worship, will be socially ostracized, "unable to buy or sell," as John puts it, and will eventually be put to death.

> And he had power to give life unto the image of the beast, that the image of the beast should both speak, and cause that as many as *would not worship* the image of the beast should be killed. [2]

(Revelation 13:15)

The prophet Daniel provides critical insight into the government of antichrist, identifying his government as a confederation of ten *kings* arising out of the Roman Empire.

> And after threescore and two weeks shall Messiah be cut off, but not for Himself: and the *people of the prince that shall come* shall destroy the city and the sanctuary; and the end thereof shall be with a flood, and unto the end of the war desolations are determined. [3]

(Daniel 9:26)

The "city and the sanctuary" referenced by Daniel are Jerusalem and the Temple. In A.D. 70, Titus, a Roman *prince*, who eventually became Caesar, sacked the city of Jerusalem and destroyed the Temple.

When they burned the Temple, its ornate gold decorations melted and ran between the cracks of the burned-out shell. The Roman soldiers had to literally dismantle the Temple, block by block, in order to plunder this rich treasure, fulfilling not only Daniel's prophecy, but also that of Jesus Christ. made some forty years earlier.

> And Jesus went out, and departed from the temple: and His disciples came to Him for to shew Him the buildings of the temple. And Jesus said unto them, See ye not all these things? verily I say unto you, There shall not be left here one stone upon another, that shall not be thrown down.
>
> (Matthew 24:1-2)

The EU, although it now has 25 members, only has ten *full* members, with the rest holding either "associate" or "observer" status. It is an *economic* union whose eventual goal is to wrest economic superpower status away from the United States and assume that mantle for itself.

Two of the three pillars of the antichrist's system are already fairly obvious, then. There is a global economic system in place. And there is an existing revived form of the old Roman Empire, headed by the ten-nation confederacy of full EU member states.

But what about the false prophet?

Two Horns Like a Lamb

According to Revelation, the false prophet will have plenty of supernatural help in establishing his religious credentials. "And he doeth great wonders, so that he maketh fire come down from heaven on the earth in the sight of men..." (Revelation 13:13).

We get few clues as to the nature of the global religion, apart from it being a kind of counterfeit Christianity with compulsory membership.

"And I beheld another beast coming up out of the earth; and he had two horns like a lamb, and he spake as a dragon" (13:11). The two horns "like a lamb" is symbolic of Christianity, but his doctrine is that of the "dragon" - Satan.

"And he exerciseth all the power of the first beast before him, and causeth the earth and them which dwell therein to worship the first beast" (13:12).

The false prophet is no figurehead - John says he is co-equal to the antichrist in power, and has the authority to *order* the worship of antichrist upon pain of death.

But before he can do that, he will have to have a religion to represent. The global religious system must first exist before it can be taken over by Satan's religious representative.

This is one reason that so many Christians have decided that the Catholic Church is the false prophet's system, and that he himself is a Pope. I don't necessarily agree with that assessment, however.

The Catholic Church would never be an acceptable global religion for the billions of Muslims, Buddhists, Hindus, animists, secular humanists, pagans, occultists and other decidedly non-Christian religions, even in the post-Christian era of the Tribulation Period.

What is more likely is a new religious system that is mor inclusive, less fundamental and more acceptable to the non-Christian worldview of the Tribulation Period.

One of the consequences of the jihadist war against the West is a global review of religious fundamentalism in all its forms; Christian, Jewish, Islamic, whatever.

The global assessment is that it isn't the teachings of the Koran that is responsible for the global war on terror. It is the religious fundamentalism that is at the heart of the conflict.

To the world, the Arab-Israeli conflict is the product of a clash between Jewish fundamentalists who believe God ceded the land to them, and the Islamic fundamentalists who believe Allah gave it to them.

Exacerbating the problem are the Christian "fundamentalists"; extremists whose religious convictions are responsible for Islam's declaration of war in the first place.

The Outlawed Gospel

Bawa Jain, secretary-general of the Millennium Peace Summit, addressed the UN's *Millennium Peace Summit of Religious and Spiritual Leaders* in New York in August, 2000. He told the assembled delegates that religions need to accept the validity of all beliefs to attain world peace.

Noted *Insight Magazine* at the time about the Summit's intention;

> According to Francis Cardinal Arinze, president for inter-religious dialogue at the Vatican and a speaker at the summit, the Catholic Church also would favor one religion in the world - if it were Roman Catholicism.

> Assorted grand muftis and other true believers hold the same view, again so long as it is their faith that is universally recognized. That each is out to convert the world is to be expected, so the proposed ban on proselytizing is surprising.[4]

With the financial backing of such heavyweights as media mogul Ted Turner and Canadian billionaire Maurice Strong, this interfaith movement has had no shortage of cash.

Turner, the honorary chairman of the peace summit, addressed the 1,000 delegates on the second morning of the convention after being praised by Strong as the man who has done more for peace, the environment and the United Nations than any other.

Episcopal Bishop William Swing gathered 300 people representing thirty-nine religions for a charter signing in Pittsburgh, officially launching the URI. This group is an anticipated melting pot of religious belief, for which a 1998 draft charter declared that all religions draw their wisdom from one ultimate source.

In 1995 Swing said the world is moving toward "unity in terms of global economy, global media and global ecological system. What is missing is a global soul."

Among Swing's goals are:

> ...a godly cease-fire, a temporary truce where the absolute exclusive claims of each [religion] will be honored but an agreed-upon neutrality will be exercised in terms of proselytizing, condemning, murdering or dominating. These will not be tolerated in the United Religions zone.[5]

We now have the complete outline: A revived Rome, an interdependent and truly global economic system, and a proposed United Religions zone.

When the prophet Daniel was given his vision of the last days, he was troubled to his core. He writes:

> And I heard, but I understood not: then said I, O my Lord, what shall be the end of these things? And he said, Go thy way, Daniel: for the words are closed up and sealed *till the time of the end.* Many shall be purified, and made white, and tried; but the wicked shall do wickedly: and none of the wicked shall understand; but the wise shall understand. [6]

(Daniel 12:8-10)

The Year of the Countdown

Consider this for a minute; but I suggest you sit down before you do.

We are so close to that system today that the *same method* is *already* being used to rout out and destroy terrorist cells! Every economic transaction, every internet session, every email and every phone call - world-wide - is already being electronically monitored as part of the war on terror.

To catch the terrorists in our midst, they must be isolated from mainstream society, their sources of funding targeted and destroyed, and their ability to engage in day-to-day social intercourse electronically interrupted.

Such intimate control of society was impossible before the advent of the Computer Age. Although there were clunky working computers dating back to the 1930's, they relied on notoriously unreliable vacuum tubes. Just firing up one of these early computing behemoths consumed enough electricity to light a small city.

The Last Generation

Bell Labs patented the transistor in 1948, launching the modern computer Age.

Before the digital explosion, transistors were a vital part of improvements in existing analog systems, such as radios and stereos.

When placed in computers, however, transistors became an integral part of the technology boom. They are capable of being mass-produced by the millions on a sliver of silicon—the semiconductor chip. It is this almost boundless ability to integrate transistors onto chips that has fueled the information age.

Today these chips are not just a part of computers. They are also important in devices as diverse as video cameras, cellular phones, copy machines, jumbo jets, automobiles, manufacturing equipment, electronic scoreboards, and video games. Without the transistor there would be no Internet and no space travel.

Revelation 13 also highlights the career of the False Prophet, who will lead a global religious system that John describes as "having two horns like a lamb" but "spake as a dragon."

The World Council of Churches, the UN-backed ecumenical movement, whose stated goal is to bring about a global religious system, was created in Amsterdam in August, 1948.

Ostensibly a *Christian* council, the WCC doctrinal statement says, it passes "no judgment upon the sincerity with which member churches accept" the WCC's basic "confession" of Jesus Christ. In other words, *not* believing in Jesus is no barrier to membership in the WCC; something Paul called, "… having a form of godliness, but denying the power thereof" (II Timothy 3).

The modern European super state traces its roots to the 1948 Benelux Treaty that inspired the modern revival of the old Roman Empire.

And finally, we return to Israel. In Leviticus 26:3, 7-8, the Bible says that the army of Israel would have a supernatural power to prevail during times of conflict. Leviticus says that five people would be able to chase away one-hundred people, and that one-hundred would chase away ten-thousand.

On May 15, 1948, Egypt, Syria, Jordan, Iraq, and Lebanon invaded Israel. The combined population of these countries was at least 20 million at the time, versus less than a million Israelis.

When the war was over, not only had Israel driven off the invaders, but she expanded her territory by over fifty percent. The 1967 war lasted only six days and left Israel in control of Jerusalem for the first time in 2000 years. The 1973 Yom Kippur War was over in a couple of weeks.

The Oil Standard

Until the early twentieth century, economic inflation was virtually unknown in the United States. In terms of purchasing power, an 1800 dollar was worth only sixty-seven cents in 1900.

That is to say, what cost a dollar in 1800 cost only sixty-seven cents a hundred years later. Rather than losing value, the purchasing power of a US dollar went up thirty-three cents in the nineteenth century.

This trend reversed over the course of the twentieth century. Although the US grew wealthier and more powerful, eclipsing the economies of every other nation early in the century, the US dollar's purchasing power began a steady decline.

What cost a dollar in 1900 now costs $21.15.

So, what happened? Early in the twentieth century, the Congress authorized the creation of the Federal Reserve Banking System to serve as America's central bank. Uniquely, the Federal Reserve was not created as a US-owned central bank, but rather, is made up of a consortium of banks, most of them foreign owned.

We've discussed the conspiracy theories about the motives behind the creation of the Federal Reserve in a previous chapter. What is relevant to this topic is how its creation and subsequent use triggered the law of unintended consequences facing our economy today.

Until the Great Depression, the US dollar was tied to gold, as it had been since the passage of the Currency Act of 1793. A dollar was redeemable in gold, and therefore, the supply of dollars was finite.

In the 1920's, the Federal Reserve began issuing more dollars than there was gold on hand to back them to finance the booming stock market. When the market crashed in 1929, the inflation and ballooning government deficits put more dollars into circulation than there was gold to redeem them.

President Franklin Roosevelt ordered all privately-held gold to be confiscated to satisfy existing creditors and the Banking Act of 1933 severed the link between gold and the US dollar.

After the outbreak of World War Two, America became the armory to the world, selling weapons to the Allies worth billions of dollars; for which it demanded payment in gold. By war's end, the majority of the world's gold reserves were back in the United States.

The *Bretton Woods Agreement* in 1945 made the US dollar convertible to gold at the government level. This established the US dollar as the world's reserve currency. The twin wars on poverty and in Vietnam drained the US economy, forcing the Fed to increase the money supply, most of which ended up as foreign reserve currency holdings.

Runaway inflation, caused by the artificial increase in the money supply, began to worry investors. By the 1970's, foreign governments began demanding payment for their dollars in gold. On August 15, 1971, the US announced it was "severing the link between the dollar and gold" and defaulted on its payments.

In order to keep the dollar (and the global economy) from collapsing, the US had to find some economic replacement for the gold standard. In 1973, Washington cut an iron-clad deal with the Saudis. The US would prop up the Saudi regime in exchange for a Saudi pledge to accept only US dollars in payment for oil. The other OPEC member nations eventually followed suit.

The nations of the world had to buy oil. And since they could only buy it with US dollars, they needed to continue to hold US dollars in reserve.

This explains much about why every president since Richard Nixon has paid homage to the King of Saud. And why Washington is willing to *look the other way* whenever the House of Saud gets caught with its hand in the cookie jar.

It is a symbiotic, if fragile, relationship. The House of Saud needs the United States to keep its regime in power. And the United States needs the House of Saud to keep the dollar from collapsing.

The Iranian Oil Bourse

In 2005, Iran announced the creation of what he called, the "Iranian Oil Bourse". It is based on a euro-oil-trading mechanism that naturally implies payment for oil in Euros, rather than dollars. The Iranian Oil Bourse would allow anyone willing either to buy or to sell oil for euros to transact on the exchange, thus circumventing the U.S. dollar altogether.

The Chinese and the Japanese should be especially eager to adopt the new exchange, because it will allow them to drastically lower their enormous dollar reserves and diversify with Euros, protecting themselves against the depreciating dollar.

The Russians have inherent economic interest in adopting the Euro – the bulk of their trade is with European countries, oil-exporting countries, China, and Japan. Adoption of the Euro will immediately take care of the first two blocs, and will, over time, facilitate trade with China and Japan.

The Arab oil-exporting countries will eagerly adopt the Euro as a means of diversifying against rising mountains of depreciating dollars. Just like the Russians, their trade is mostly with European countries, and therefore will prefer the European currency both for its stability and for avoiding currency risk, not to mention their jihad against the US.

Hugo Chavez, who now sits atop the world's largest proven oil reserves, announced that Venezuela was ready to move his country's foreign-exchange holdings out of the dollar and into the euro.

All Roads Lead To Rome

In spite of the skyrocketing economy, the value of the US dollar it is based on continues to decline in value against other currencies, especially the euro. And, for the first time since the World War One, the value of the European stock market has passed that of the United States.

European market capitalization rose to $1.57 trillion, passing the US market value of $1.56 trillion. European market shares are outperforming US market shares by nearly a two to one margin. And since 2003, the euro has risen 26 percent against the dollar.

Blast from the (Recent) Past

Back in 1969, Hal Lindsey wrote in _The Late Great Planet Earth_ that he believed something had to happen in the near future, if indeed these are the last days as foretold by Scripture.

Somehow, he said, _something_ had to happen to cause the decline or fall of both the Soviet Union and the United States.

The Bible's outline demands a revived form of the old Roman Empire co-exist with a Jewish state called "Israel" in the last days.   ·'

The Bible predicts the final form of world government would be headquartered in Rome, not Moscow or Washington.

Remember, in 1969, America was at the height of its power and the Cold War was at its hottest. Western Europe was still struggling with post war reconstruction and Eastern Europe was firmly under the heel of Soviet domination.

The Last Generation

The idea of a European super state rising to eclipse both the United States and the Soviet Union in our lifetime was laughable.

But the Bible says that the same generation to witness the restoration of Israel would see the revival of the old Roman Empire, the annihilation of Russia at the head of a Persian-led Islamic confederation on the mountains of Israel and says nothing at all about the existence of a global superpower resembling the United States of America.

EPILOGUE

Knowing is *Not* Believing

There are many alive today who believe in God, and who believe the lie that knowing will make the difference when they stand before the Judge of the Universe.

Knowing God is a one sided business. For example, I know a lot about Bill Clinton. I know the names of his wife and child, his brother, father, mother and other personal details. I know when and where he was born, a lot about his personal philosophy and his political worldview. I even know how much money he made last year.

But, for all that, Bill Clinton doesn't know me! If I passed him on the street, I could say, "Hi Bill". But I'd be kidding myself if I thought he'd say, "Hi Jack," in reply.

The Apostle James wrote; "Thou believest that there is one God; thou doest well: the devils also believe, and tremble" (James 2:19). He makes a valid point.

Satan believes in God; he's spoken with Him, face to face. But Satan isn't going to heaven! Neither will the rest of the angels that rebelled with him. The Bible tells us that the lake of fire is a place prepared for the devil and his angels.

Those who think believing in God is all they need to ensure that they will spend eternity in heaven would do well to heed the warning contained in Matthew 7:22-23.

> Many will say to me in that day, Lord, Lord, have we not prophesied in thy name? and in thy name have cast out devils? and in thy name done many wonderful works? And then will I profess unto them, I never knew you: depart from me, ye that work iniquity.

Nearly every person on earth who knows of the United States; but that doesn't make them US citizens.

It isn't *believing* in God that grants a person heavenly citizenship, but rather an intimate *relationship with* Him through Jesus Christ.

What Must I Do?

The Bible says that all human beings are born with an eternal citizenship. That citizenship is in the kingdom of Satan, and their ultimate home is the place reserved for that kingdom - the lake of fire.

Romans 3:23 says "For all have sinned, and come short of the glory of God." No matter how good a person one might be, everyone has sinned, at least once. That sin demands judgment.

The Bible says that "the wages of sin is death" (Romans 6:23), and God is a righteous God. He will pay the wages due each person.

By way of analogy, imagine you are on trial for murder. Your defense attorney says, "My client did commit this murder, but since then, he has been a model citizen. He gave all he has to the poor, helps old ladies across the street, discovered a cure for cancer, and invented a better mousetrap."

Those good works have no bearing on the central issue - that you are guilty of the crime for which you have been charged. God's justice is at least as fair as man's. Yet we somehow are willing to accept the lie that He is willing to "bend the law" in our case. The truth is, He will not, and cannot "bend the law" and remain a Righteous Judge.

The judge in our hypothetical case cannot ignore the issue of guilt or innocence, but he can modify the punishment. Again, God reserves the same right to Himself.

We are all guilty, and we stand convicted of our sins before Him. Jesus said; "He that believeth on him [Jesus] is not condemned: but he that believeth not is condemned already;" (John 3:18).

In popular parlance, the term "born again" is usually reserved for the rabid *lunatic fringe* type of Christian. But, if we are to accept the Bible as true, then that is the only definition of a Christian.

This is not my doctrine, or the doctrine of a particular denomination or sect. It is the stated doctrine of Jesus Christ, from Whom we derive the name *Christian*.

"Jesus answered and said unto him, Verily, verily, I say unto thee, Except a man be born again, he cannot see the kingdom of God" (John 3:3).

And again: "Marvel not that I said unto thee, Ye *must* be born again" (John 3:7).[1]

Without this "born again" experience, Jesus Christ says a man cannot see the kingdom of God. If Heaven is His kingdom, and a person must go there to see it, then a person who is not born again can't go there. Go ahead, mull on that, and see if you can interpret it differently.

Now for the good news. The "born again" experience is available to anyone who asks for it. So is eternity in

Heaven. You don't have to "prepare" yourself in advance and you don't need to first clean up your life; you only need come before Jesus Christ and admit your need.

The simplicity of salvation proves to be the undoing of many who think they, in some way, have a role to play. That they have to first quit smoking, or drinking, or some other sin before they can come to Him. Time for another analogy.

You discover one of your children is missing in the woods. You call out the police, the neighborhood watch, the National Guard, and you begin the search. After a week or so, the search is called off - but you keep looking. You spend each day searching every possible hiding place. At last - you see your missing child across the pasture. You run to each other. Music swells in the background, and everything turns to slow motion.

Just as you are about to embrace your lost child, you stop! You notice he is dirty and smelly from his time lost in the woods.

Before you embrace him, you scold him and tell him to take a bath and clean himself up. Then you'll resume the reunion. ??? That makes no sense, does it?

Jesus Christ loves each of us with a love so intense, so personal, and so forgiving that He was willing to pay the price for our sins.

He allowed His own creation to seize Him for crimes he did not commit, to abuse and mutilate Him, and to exact from Him the wages of our sin - a criminal's death.

Can anything we do *add* to that payment? Would He then expect more from us, for whom He died, than we would expect from our own lost child?

230

When Jesus embraces a sinner He is embracing a lost child, whom He loves beyond our comprehension. He doesn't care what sins stain us, He only sees a child who was lost, and now is found.

Like the human parent in our analogy, He first joyfully embraces His lost one. Then He takes responsibility for the clean up job.

If you have read this far, by now you must recognize that something is going on in our world that defies every conventional explanation. But it fits perfectly with the revealed Word of God. All the things God said would happen are happening. Those things yet to come will be fulfilled with the same precision.

Nothing will be overlooked. And that includes the judgment. Which side will you be on? Won't you allow Christ to embrace you as His child? Right now, right where you are, you can seal your eternal destiny.

Ask Jesus to accept you as you are and forgive you of your sins. Change your mind about your sin and allow Him to make changes in your mind and your heart.

"Being confident of this very thing, that He which hath begun a good work in you will perform it until the day of Jesus Christ:" (Philippians 1:6).

A New Life

That's all there is to it! You are a Christian. No matter what, regardless of what anyone else does or says to you, you have eternal life, according to the Bible. Eternal life, by definition, is eternal!

You cannot lose it, or it would not be eternal! Jesus promised; "And I give unto them eternal life; and they shall never perish, neither shall any man pluck them out of my hand" (John 10:28).

Jesus holds me in the palm of His Hand. I am a man. If I could therefore do anything that could negate this promise, then Jesus lied. No man can pluck me from His Hand, including me.

If you have turned your life over to Him for safekeeping, then the same applies to you. You are an adopted son of God, with full family membership. Welcome to the family! I look forward to seeing you in Heaven.

Nothing, or Everything to Lose

On the other hand, if you reject God's offer of pardon, then by the authority of the Word of God, you will not enter into Heaven, but will spend eternity in the lake of fire, alone, nameless, and sharing in the torment God prepared for Satan himself!

There is no middle of the road. I pray you will reconsider. Eternal life is free. There is no charge for admission. I gain nothing that can be measured in this lifetime by your acceptance or rejection of the Gospel.

I'll take it one step further. Let's argue that I am wrong. The Bible is not true, and there is nothing after this life but the grave. What have I lost by accepting Jesus Christ? In the end, I will be just as dead as you. Embracing Christianity will not change my life, because it isn't real. So I risk nothing.

But, what if you are wrong? What if everything I have presented is true? What if there is an afterlife? By accepting Jesus Christ, I have lost nothing.

By rejecting Jesus Christ, you have lost eternity.

END NOTES

CHAPTER ONE – THE RESTORATION OF ISRAEL

[1] The Scotsman, November 21, 2006,
http://thescotsman.scotsman.com/index.cfm?id=1720952006

[2] *Personal Witness,* Abba Eban, p. 144

[3] emphasis author's

[4] "Did the Jews Live in Ancient Israel?"
http://www.hyperhistory.net/apwh/essays/others/tahrifi-lafzi.htm

[5] ibid

[6] emphasis author's

[7] emphasis author's

CHAPTER TWO – THE ALIGNMENT OF NATIONS

[1] Antiquities of the Jews, I:6.

[2] Antiquities of the Jews I:6.

[3] emphasis author's

[4] Calculations courtesy of "Evidence That Demands a Verdict" by Josh McDowell

[5] emphasis author's

CHAPTER THREE – FALSE CHRISTS

[1] http://en.wikipedia.org/wiki/Dajjal

CHAPTER FOUR – WARS AND RUMORS OF WARS

[1] "The Effects Of Nuclear War"
http://www.fas.org/nuke/intro/nuke/7906/

[2] "U.S. official: Chinese test missile obliterates satellite" – CNN
http://www.cnn.com/2007/TECH/space/01/18/china.missile/index.html (January 19, 2007)

[3] Wikipedia Online Encyclopedia,
http://en.wikipedia.org/wiki/Ballistic_missile

[4] "Red Face Over China", CNN AllPolitics,
http://www.cnn.com/ALLPOLITICS/1998/05/25/time/china.missles.html

[5] CNN All Politics "Clinton Defends China Satellite Waiver"
http://www.cnn.com/ALLPOLITICS/1998/05/22/china.money/

[6] ibid

[7] ibid

[8] GlobalSecurity.org "China's Defense Budget,"
http://www.globalsecurity.org/military/world/china/budget.htm

[9] London Telegraph, "US Condemns China's Satellite Killer Test"
January 19, 2007
http://www.telegraph.co.uk/news/main.jhtml?xml=/news/2007/01/18/wchina118.xml

[10] Geostrategy Direct http://www.geostrategydirect.com

[11] "Congress and the Case For War" Washington Post
http://blog.washingtonpost.com/thedebate/2005/12/drafting_congre.html

[12] FrontPageMagazine.com "It's Springtime For the Mahdi in Tehran" – Robert Spencer

[13] Joel C Rosenberg "Iran Sobered Us Up On New Year's" National Review Online http://article.nationalreview.com/?q=Nzc1YTNjZDlmZjU3MzBjMT NhMjFhNDNmYjNmNjU0NTI=

[1] Milwaukee Journal – Sentinel May 16, 2006

[2] emphasis author's

CHAPTER FIVE - DECEIVED

[3] "CNN Knew" -The Omega Letter Archives, http://www.omegaletter.com/files/CNN_Knew_The_Washington_Times.htm

[4] http://www.newsroom.ucla.edu/page.asp?RelNum=6664

CHAPTER SIX – EARTHQUAKES, FAMINES AND PESTILENCES

[1] AIDS Will Cause Negative Population Growth, New Data Shows: USAID presents population impact of disease" – US Information Agency http://www.aegis.com/news/usis/2000/US000705.html

[2] FDA "Bad Bug Book" http://www.cfsan.fda.gov/~mow/chap15.html

[3] JAMA, January 18, 1995 "Global Tuberculosis Mortality 1990-2000", http://lib.bioinfo.pl/pmid:8205640

[4] CDC Fact Sheet http://www.cdc.gov/ncidod/dpd/parasites/cryptosporidiosis/factsht_cryptosporidiosis.htm

[5] "Deaths From Hepatitis C" http://www.wrongdiagnosis.com/h/hepatitis_c/deaths.htm

[6] "America's Forgotten Pandemic" – Alfred W. Crosby – Cambridge University Press, 2nd Edition

[7] CDC Fact Sheet http://www.cdc.gov/flu/avian/gen-info/facts.htm

[8] USDA http://www.fda.gov/ola/2005/influenza0504.html

[9] WHO EPR Report http://www.who.int/csr/disease/avian_influenza/avian_faqs/en/index.html

[10] "Rise of Deadly Superbugs Should "Raise Red Flags Everywhere" Live Science http://www.livescience.com/humanbiology/050509_superbugs.html

[11] Medical News Today, "Two Studies Document Rise of Superbugs in the Environment" http://www.medicalnewstoday.com/medicalnews.php?newsid=24093

[12] Scientific American, "The Scarred Earth" http://scientificamerican.com/article.cfm?chanID=sa004&articleID=000EA704-9479-1213-947983414B7F0000

[13] USGS "Are Earthquakes Really on the Increase?" http://earthquake.usgs.gov/learning/topics/increase_in_earthquakes.php

[14] Matthew 24:7, emphasis author's

[15] Science Daily "Only 10% of Fish Left in Global Ocean" http://www.sciencedaily.com/releases/2003/05/030515075848.htm

[16] ibid

[17] "Doomsday Vault to Avert World Famine" January 12, 2006 http://www.newscientist.com/article.ns?id=mg18925343.700)

[18] http://www.museumofhoaxes.com/hoax/forums/viewthread/3028/

CHAPTER SEVEN – SUN, MOON, STARS

[1] http://news.bbc.co.uk/2/hi/science/nature/2166598.stm

[2] http://www.cbc.ca/quirks/archives/02-03/dec07.html

[3]
http://observer.guardian.co.uk/international/story/0,6903,750783,00.html, Guardian Unlimited, July 7, 2002

[4] Guardian Unlimited, "Two-Thirds of World's Resources Used Up" March 30, 2005
http://www.guardian.co.uk/international/story/0,3604,1447863,00.html

[5] WorldNet daily, September 23, 2004
http://www.worldnetdaily.com/news/article.asp?ARTICLE_ID=40584

[6] ibid

[7] William Broad, NYTimes: Will Compasses Point South?
http://www.nytimes.com/2004/07/13/science/13magn.html

[8]
http://www.space.com/scienceastronomy/solar_storms_sun_040708.html

[9] bulletin number 658; 2000

[10]
http://www.munichre.com/en/press/press_releases/2000/2000_02_29_press_release.aspx

[11] emphasis author's

[12] emphasis author's

CHAPTER EIGHT – THE REVIVED ROMAN EMPIRE

[1] From the Western European Alliance's official website:
http://www.weu.int/

CHAPTER NINE – GLOBAL ECONOMY

[1] Quoted from "The Creature on Jekyll Island," attributed to Frank Vanderlip, "Farm Boy to Financier," Saturday Evening Post, February 8, 1935

[2] emphasis author's

CHAPTER TEN – THE MARK OF THE BEAST

[1] USAToday, "Will That Be Cash, Fingerprint or Cell Phone?" Keven Maney, November 16, 2003

[2] emphasis author's

[3] emphasis author's

[4] Insight Magazine, "U.N. Faithful Eye Global Religion" October 2, 2000

[5] http://www.orthodoxanglican.org/TCC/stories/looknow.txt

[6] emphasis author's

EPILOGUE

[1] emphasis author's

"My wife introduced me to the Omega Letter in 2001. Jack's analyses of current events and their correlation with Bible prophecy soon had me hooked."
Craig
Crocker, Missouri

"I look forward every morning reading Jack's briefing. It and the members' discussions are the highlight of my days."
Trudy
Missouri

"The Omega letter has become my first port of call when I log onto the internet. Jack's analysis is always relevant witty and insightful. I couldn't be without it."
Alf
Melbourne, Australia

"The OL has changed our life; we have received prayer support, encouragement, correction, and so much love! To us, the OL is a bit of heaven on earth."
Ken and Georgia
Tomball, Texas

"The Omega Letter is so much more than a publication and a forum. It is a living church with Jesus Christ at its center."
Sue
Salinas, CA

"I find myself making the Omega Letter the first reading for the day. What a great way to start off the day with Jack's encouragements, wit and latest news reports and comments."
Brad
Des Moines, IA